S0-ADK-790

BATTLESHIPS
OF WORLD WAR II

**ROGERS MEMORIAL
LIBRARY**

ROGERS MEMORIAL
LIBRARY

BATTLESHIPS
OF WORLD WAR II

AN ILLUSTRATED HISTORY AND COUNTRY-BY-COUNTRY DIRECTORY OF WARSHIPS THAT FOUGHT IN
THE SECOND WORLD WAR AND BEYOND, INCLUDING BATTLECRUISERS AND POCKET BATTLESHIPS

PETER HORE

southwater

This edition is published by Southwater
an imprint of Anness Publishing Ltd
Hermes House
88–89 Blackfriars Road
London SE1 8HA
tel. 020 7401 2077; fax 020 7633 9499

www.southwaterbooks.com; www.annesspublishing.com

Anness Publishing has a new picture agency outlet for images for publishing, promotions or advertising.
Please visit our website www.practicalpictures.com for more information.

UK agent: The Manning Partnership Ltd, 6 The Old Dairy,
Melcombe Road, Bath BA2 3LR; tel. 01225 478444;
fax 01225 478440; sales@manning-partnership.co.uk

UK distributor: Grantham Book Services Ltd, Isaac Newton Way,
Alma Park Industrial Estate, Grantham, Lincs NG31 9SD
tel. 01476 541080; fax 01476 541061; orders@gbs.tbs-ltd.co.uk

North American agent/distributor: National Book Network,
4501 Forbes Boulevard, Suite 200, Lanham, MD 20706
tel. 301 459 3366; fax 301 429 5746; www.nbnbooks.com

Australian agent/distributor: Pan Macmillan Australia,
Level 18, St Martins Tower,
31 Market St,
Sydney, NSW 2000
tel. 1300 135 113; fax 1300 135 103;
customer.service@macmillan.com.au

New Zealand agent/distributor: David Bateman Ltd,
30 Tarndale Grove, Off Bush Road,
Albany, Auckland
tel. (09) 415 7664; fax (09) 415 8892

Publisher: Joanna Lorenz
Senior Managing Editor: Conor Kilgallon
Senior Editor: Felicity Forster
Copy Editor and Indexer: Tim Ellerby
Cover Design: Jonathan Davison
Designer: Ian Sandom
Production Controller: Don Campaniello

ETHICAL TRADING POLICY

At Anness Publishing we believe that business should be conducted in an ethical and ecologically sustainable way, with respect for the environment and a proper regard to the replacement of the natural resources we employ. As a publisher, we use a lot of high-quality paper for printing, mostly made from spruce trees. We are therefore currently growing more than 500,000 trees in two Scottish forest plantations near Aberdeen – Berrymoss (130 hectares/320 acres) and West Touxhill (125 hectares/305 acres). The forests we manage contain twice the number of trees employed each year in paper-making for our books. Because of this ongoing ecological investment programme, you, as our customer, can have the pleasure and reassurance of knowing that a tree is being cultivated on your behalf to naturally replace the materials used to make the book you are holding. Our forestry programme is run in accordance with the UK Woodland Assurance Scheme (UKWAS) and will be certified by the internationally recognized Forest Stewardship Council (FSC). The FSC is a non-government organization dedicated to promoting responsible management of the world's forests. Certification ensures forests are managed in an environmentally sustainable and socially responsible way. For further information about this scheme, go to www.annesspublishing.com/trees.

© Anness Publishing Ltd 2007

All rights reserved. No part of this publication may be reproduced, stored in a retrieval
system, or transmitted in any way or by any means, electronic, mechanical, photocopying,
recording or otherwise, without the prior written permission of the copyright holder.

A CIP catalogue record for this book is available from the British Library.

Previously published as part of a larger volume, *Battleships*

1 3 5 7 9 10 8 6 4 2

PAGE 1: **USS *Alabama*.** PAGES 2–3: **USS *North Carolina*.** PAGE 5: ***Deutschland (Lützow).***

Contents

Introduction

A basic style of sailing ship, capable of taking part in battles – or a "line-of-battle ship", from which the term "battleship" is derived – dominated warfare at sea from the 16th to the 19th century. Then, just as the British Navy celebrated her sea victory in 1805 at the Battle of Trafalgar, new technology became available which revolutionized battleship design. This revolution encompassed the use of steam engines at sea, breech-loading guns, the rotating turret, armour and above all the increase in size of ships. At one stage a British prime minister complained that ship design was a changing fashion like ladies' hats.

The battleship itself, broadly defined here as a capital ship mounting guns of 255mm/10in calibre or more, took on many different shapes for the first 20 years of its life. Designers faced difficult choices, weight being a primary driver in the decisions which had to be made. For example, many early designs had large, heavy barbettes, which meant a low freeboard and loss of sea-keeping; the alternative was a high-sided ship with a resulting loss of stability. This period was marked by some exceedingly odd and ugly ships.

There were developmental dead ends as well. The paddle ship, with its exposed wheels, was useless as a vehicle of war – the paddlewheels and boxes were too vulnerable to damage and restricted the size of broadside armament that could be mounted. However, the paddle ship was useful for towing sailing ships into action.

TOP: **HMS *Ramillies* in 1943, with a disruptive camouflage scheme.**
ABOVE: **The *Yamato*, under construction, showing off one of her huge 455mm/18in guns. Battleships of this class were the largest ever built.**

Other lines of development took unexpected turns. The monitor was designed for coastal defence and for war in estuaries and rivers, and was highly successful in the American Civil War. However, when given a little more sea-keeping capability, monitors became powerful weapons of offence, mounting some of the largest guns taken from their "big sister" battleships. In two World Wars, monitors were used in operations from the Arctic to Africa, and indeed at the end of their lives the shore-bombardment role of some battleships could be compared to that of an over-large monitor.

By the end of the 19th century the design of the battleship had more or less settled on a ship of about 10,160 tonnes/

ABOVE: **The sleek lines of the** **_Scharnhorst_ can be clearly** **seen. Her brief life as a** **commerce raider tied up a** **great deal of British naval** **assets until she was finally** **sunk in December 1943.**
LEFT: **Big-gun ships still** **needed to be protected** **against smaller craft.**
RIGHT: **Each shell was the** **size of a man.**

10,000 tons, carrying two twin barbettes or turrets, one forward and one aft, and sometimes with side-by-side funnels. Their speed of 18 knots was considered fast.

Then, a British admiral, Jacky Fisher, changed everything with his concept of a battleship which would "dread nought". It was not his idea alone. The Italian naval engineer Vittorio Cuniberti's proposals for an all-big-gun ship were widely published, and there were simultaneous developments in the same direction in several other countries as well. However, it was Fisher's energy, enthusiasm and drive which brought the first ship, HMS _Dreadnought_, into being, and halted warship-building worldwide, while allies and enemies considered the implications. Although the design was not perfect, the ship was revolutionary in nearly every respect, and thereafter battleships were classified by reference to this one ship, as pre-Dreadnoughts, Dreadnoughts or super-Dreadnoughts.

Once the 20,320-tonne/20,000-ton and 20-knot barrier had been broken, development continued apace, and within 10 years, subsequent generations of Dreadnoughts had reached 30,480 tonnes/30,000 tons and 30 knots. Eventually the largest ships of this type exceeded 60,960 tonnes/ 60,000 tons. Secondary armament was re-introduced to deal with torpedo boats and later for anti-aircraft use. Triple and even quadruple turrets were fitted, along with ramps

and then catapults for aircraft, and oil replaced coal. Reciprocating engines were replaced by steam turbines and in some cases by diesel engines.

Unlike in World War I and the pre-Dreadnought periods, there were no major fleet engagements involving battleships during World War II, although there were a number of fiercely fought smaller actions. Battleships were soon relegated to auxiliary roles such as forming an anti-aircraft screen to defend aircraft carriers and for shore bombardment in support of amphibious landings. By the end of World War II the type was all but obsolete, although in the US Navy the battleship lingered on, seeing action in various hot spots around the world, most notably in the Korean and Vietnam Wars, and finally in the 1990–91 Gulf War.

This book looks first at the fascinating history of the battleship covering the period from the end of World War I up to the last actions in the Gulf War in 1991. It also chronicles the main battles and naval operations of the period mounted by the world's foremost naval powers, notably Britain, the United States, Germany, France, Italy and Japan. The country-by-country directory that follows describes the most famous and important battleships of the time. This, then, is the story, told through the lives of individual ships, of the final period of development, deployment and demise of one type of ship which dominated naval strategy for 150 years.

The History of World War II Battleships

The term battleship derives from "line-of-battle ship", meaning a ship strong enough to fight in the line of battle. However, by the beginning of World War II it was apparent that large fleet engagements were largely a thing of the past. Submarine warfare was now well developed and the devastating effectiveness of attacks by aircraft on unprotected surface vessels was about to be demonstrated.

As the war progressed, battleships were increasingly marginalized and assigned the secondary roles of land bombardment and anti-aircraft protection for the carrier fleets.

There were still some epic surface engagements involving battleships, such as the sinking of the *Hood* and the search for the *Bismarck*, but these were few in number and usually involved aircraft and submarine action.

After World War II, the remaining battleships were quickly decommissioned and scrapped, with the notable exception of those in the US fleet. A number of battleships were preserved as museum ships and four *Iowa*-class battleships were retained in reserve, seeing intermittent service up to the end of the Gulf War in 1991.

LEFT: **A view taken onboard a US battleship of the New Mexico class during the capture of Saipan in 1944. A sister ship follows next astern and the USS *Pennsylvania* completes the line ahead.**

The naval treaties

There were a number of international treaties that attempted to limit naval armaments, including the size and number of battleships. At the end of World War I the most modern units of the German High Seas Fleet had been interned at Scapa Flow, where they were scuttled in 1919, and Britannia, or rather the Royal Navy, once more ruled the waves. However, Japan, which had been following a British naval tradition and an ally since the Anglo-Japanese Treaty of 1902, and the USA, which had sent a squadron of battleships to join the Grand Fleet at Scapa Flow, represented new challenges.

The 1916 US Naval Program had called for ten battleships and six battlecruisers, which would give the United States Navy (USN) a fleet of modern battleships. In contrast, all the Royal Navy's battleships, except *Hood,* which was still incomplete, were pre-war. The Japanese also had a battleship-building programme, as did France and Italy. Then in November 1921, US President Harding convened a naval disarmament conference in Washington.

To the surprise of the British, the USA offered to scrap much of the 1916 and later programmes, and proposed a ten-year holiday on new construction. Specifically, the USA proposed that a ratio should be agreed for the number of ships which should be scrapped, and that the number of battleships retained by each nation should be used to calculate the numbers of other warships each nation could keep. Battleships would only be replaced when they were 20 years old and then they could not exceed 35,560 tonnes/35,000 tons standard displacement (the displacement of a ship fully equipped for sea except for fuel).

TOP: **USN warships being scrapped at Philadelphia in the 1920s. On the right is the battleship *Maine* (down by the bows) and centre (with her cage masts still in place) is the battleship *Wisconsin*. The Washington Naval Treaty caused the world's fleets to be culled.** ABOVE: **The first of a series of interwar naval conferences was staged in Washington in this specially converted theatre, where the delegates knew that they had the opportunity to make history.**

After weeks of negotiation, a formula was agreed of British to American to Japanese battleships in the ratio of 5:5:3, and to limit battleship guns to 405m/16in. A separate Four Power Treaty, which included France, attempted to neutralize the Western Pacific and ended the period of Anglo-Japanese cooperation. France and Italy were given smaller ratios, but France obtained parity in submarine numbers with Britain and the USA. The tonnage and gun size of cruisers was also limited, but not the number, Britain insisting that she needed large numbers of cruisers for the protection of Empire trade. The size of aircraft carriers was set at a maximum of 27,500 tonnes/27,000 tons, and the total tonnage was agreed for Britain and the USA as 35,560 tonnes/35,000 tons each, Japan 82,300 tonnes/81,000 tons, and France and Italy as 61,000 tonnes/60,000 tons each.

The Washington Naval Treaty of 1922, which seemed to have curtailed Anglo-American rivalry while making it impossible for Japan to challenge the USA in the Pacific, was to be effective for 15 years. Several issues remained unresolved but a subsequent naval arms limitation conference at Geneva in 1927 was not successful and France and Italy refused to attend. The British wanted to revise the Washington Treaty to allow 30,500-tonne/30,000-ton battleships with 340mm/13.5in guns. Britain and the USA disagreed about the number of cruisers that should be allowed – the USA wanted parity at 254,000–305,000 tonnes/250,000–300,000 tons for all cruisers. However, the Royal Navy thought it needed over 406,500 tonnes/400,000 tons for the defence of the Empire, and Japan wanted a limit on heavy, 205mm/8in-gun cruisers. The British hoped to set a new limit on the tonnage of submarines. However, the conference formally broke up without agreement though desultory talks continued, while the USA endeavoured to build cruisers to match those of the Royal Navy.

The controversy about cruisers continued at the London Conference of 1930. The Royal Navy conceded a limit of 25,400 tonnes/25,000 tons standard displacement and 305mm/12in guns, and the life was extended to 26 years. This was not accepted, but the numbers of battleships were reduced to a ratio of 15:15:9. A second London Conference was convened in 1935 at which Britain and the USA refused to grant parity to Japan, as this would have given her local superiority in the Far East. Japan then gave notice that she would withdraw from the original Washington Treaty, and Italy followed suit. The main benefit of this conference was the agreement signed by Britain, France and the USA that provided for notice to be given of intended construction. Italy, Germany, Poland and the Soviet Union later assented to this.

TOP: **The Japanese delegation, which came to Washington in 1921, included Count Shidehara (second left) and Admiral Kato. They were disappointed not to achieve parity with Britain and the USA.** ABOVE: **The guns of scrapped warships photographed lying in Philadelphia Navy Yard in 1923.**

Battleship numbers in 1939

COUNTRY	IN SERVICE	UNDER CONSTRUCTION
Britain	15	5
France	7	4
Germany	5	4
Italy	4	4
Japan	10	4
USA	15	8
Total	56	29

In 1935, Britain also agreed to an Anglo-German Naval Agreement that allowed Germany 35 per cent of the British tonnage in all classes of warships.

The Indian Ocean

The World War II battleship campaign in the Indian Ocean is one of the least known and studied, but nevertheless features many key aspects of battleship warfare. Two German surface raiders visited the Indian Ocean: the pocket battleship *Graf Spee* in October 1939, where she claimed a small tanker of 717 tonnes/706 tons south-west of Madagascar and then escaped back into the South Atlantic before Anglo-French hunting groups could find her, and the pocket battleship *Admiral Scheer,* which reached as far as the Seychelles in spring 1941 and was lucky to evade the hunting British cruisers. The purpose of these raids was to cause British and allied warships to disperse and to make them introduce the convoy system, which the Germans regarded as inefficient. However these raids were so short-lived that they had little effect on the actual distribution and deployment of Allied warships.

Until 1942, however, the Indian Ocean remained a relatively safe theatre of operations for the Royal Navy. Admiral Sir James Somerville, who had successfully commanded the battleships and aircraft carriers of Force H based at Gibraltar, had been sent to command a new Eastern Fleet based in Ceylon (Sri Lanka). Somerville formed his fleet in two groups, a fast division consisting of the battleship *Warspite* and two carriers, *Indomitable* and *Formidable*, and a slow division composed of the four battleships *Resolution, Ramillies, Royal Sovereign* and *Revenge*, and the carrier *Hermes*. Both

ABOVE: *Warspite* **formed part of the fast division of Admiral Somerville's Eastern Fleet as he manoeuvred to avoid succumbing to superior Japanese naval power.** BELOW: **The slow division of Somerville's fleet comprised four elderly battleships, including** *Ramillies,* **which would have been no match for Nagumo's carriers. Thousands of men were engaged, and put at risk, in this strategic deployment.**

Colombo and Trincomalee were poorly defended and Somerville made a secret base at Addu Atoll in the Maldives.

In early April the Japanese navy struck into the Indian Ocean. A force of carriers and cruisers entered the Bay of Bengal and sank 23 ships of 113,800 tonnes/112,000 tons, while Japanese submarines attacked shipping on the west coast of India. Meanwhile a strong carrier group (the same ships as had attacked Pearl Harbor) escorted by four fast battleships reached for Ceylon. However, the Japanese admiral Nagumo lost the element of surprise when his force was sighted on April 4 south of Ceylon, and Somerville was able to clear his ships from their ports.

Between April 5 and 9 Japanese air attacks were frustrated, and only a British destroyer and an armed merchant cruiser were caught in harbour, and two heavy cruisers were discovered at sea and sunk. Somerville's aggressive spirit led him to attempt a counter-attack, and the elderly carrier *Hermes* and two of her escorts were sunk when returning to Colombo. The Japanese then left the Indian Ocean, and Somerville, uncertain of where his enemy was, retired, sending his slow group to East Africa and his fast group to Bombay. The Japanese had thus secured their perimeter and reached the high tide of their expansion for little cost in either material or ships.

The British were now concerned about further Japanese raids into the Indian Ocean and about the neutrality of Madagascar, held by the Vichy French. A large force including two carriers and the battleship *Ramillies* was assembled at Durban for Operation Ironclad, the occupation of Diego Suarez, a natural harbour at the northern end of Madagascar. There on May 30 the Japanese counter-attacked using midget submarines and *Ramillies* was severely damaged, needing to be towed back to Durban for temporary repairs.

Thereafter Somerville's Eastern Fleet was reduced to reinforce other theatres, and throughout August he carried out diversionary raids using the carrier *Illustrious* and the battleships *Warspite* and *Valiant*. From September to November 1942 the remainder of the island of Madagascar was occupied and the Indian Ocean was relatively quiet for the next year, during which Axis submarines scored some successes.

In January 1944 the British Eastern Fleet was strengthened by the arrival of *Queen Elizabeth, Valiant, Renown* and several

ABOVE: **The Japanese admiral Nagumo, who had planned and led the air strike on Pearl Harbor, hoped to catch the British in Trincomalee, but Somerville was warned and escaped to a secret anchorage.**

carriers. This was in preparation for a series of strikes against Japanese-held positions on Sumatra beginning on April 19, by which time the Eastern Fleet included the Free French battleship *Richelieu*. Thereafter the war in the Indian Ocean was increasingly prosecuted using carrier-based aircraft, and in August *Valiant* was badly damaged and never again fully repaired after the dry dock she was in collapsed.

In November 1944 the British Eastern Fleet was split into the British East Indies Fleet including the battleships *Queen Elizabeth* and *Renown*, and the British Pacific Fleet based in Australia including the battleships *Howe* and *King George V*. Aircraft carriers, however, predominated in both fleets as the battle moved out of the Indian Ocean. After World War II the Indian Ocean once more became a naval power vacuum, until the growth of the Indian navy in the late 20th century.

RIGHT: **Later in the war the British Eastern Fleet was strengthened by the deployment of fast battleships like *Valiant* and several aircraft carriers. The distances involved were huge and Trincomalee became an important staging post and centre for training for the fleet both in its attack on the Japanese-held East Indies, and in its deployment to the east of Australia, where the British Pacific Fleet would be based.**

LEFT: **The 380mm/15in guns of the battleship *Valiant* firing a broadside; astern of her are *Barham* and *Warspite*. These three ships, based at Alexandria in Egypt, formed the backbone of Cunningham's fleet.**
ABOVE: **"ABC" or Admiral Sir Andrew Cunningham, Commander-in-Chief of the British Mediterranean Fleet, was the greatest British Admiral since Nelson.**
BELOW: **The battleship *Renown* and the aircraft carrier *Ark Royal* belonged to Force H, which held the western end of the Mediterranean and could be deployed into the Atlantic.**

Cunningham and the battleship war in the Mediterranean

The actions between the British and Italian fleets in the Mediterranean in 1940–3 were some of the last involving battleship against battleship, with characteristics reminiscent of the North Sea battles of World War I and a foretaste of the carrier battles in the Pacific. The driving spirit of the British Mediterranean Fleet was "ABC" Cunningham, who in June 1939 became Commander-in-Chief, Mediterranean Fleet, and is widely regarded as the greatest admiral since Nelson.

After the fall of France, the Royal Navy's first objective was the neutralization of the French fleet. When the French turned down all British suggestions to neutralize their fleet at Mers-el-Kebir, Admiral Somerville, commanding Force H, reluctantly fired upon his former allies. The battleship *Bretagne* blew up, *Provence* and *Dunkerque* were badly damaged, but *Strasbourg* escaped to Toulon. *Dunkerque* was torpedoed a few days later by *Ark Royal*'s aircraft. At Alexandria Cunningham persuaded the French Admiral Godfrey to agree to demilitarize his flagship, *Lorraine*.

In July 1940 Cunningham sailed from Alexandria with *Warspite*, *Malaya* and *Royal Sovereign*, and the aircraft carrier *Eagle* to cover convoys in the central Mediterranean. Intelligence told Cunningham that two Italian battleships, *Giulio Cesare* and *Conte di Cavour*, were escorting a convoy to North Africa, and Cunningham changed course to cut them off. *Warspite* hit *Giulio Cesare* at extreme range and as the Italians retreated Cunningham pursued them to within sight of

Calabria, scoring a moral victory which would set the tone for the rest of this war. Off Cape Spartivento on November 27, Force H, led by Somerville in *Renown*, exchanged long-range shots with *Vittorio Veneto* and *Guilio Cesare*, but, handicapped by the slower *Ramillies*, Somerville could not close with his quarry. A few weeks later, on February 9, 1941, Somerville took *Renown*, *Malaya* and the aircraft carrier *Ark Royal* into the Gulf of Genoa to bombard and mine Genoa, Leghorn and La Spezia. This time it was the Italian fleet which was too late to catch the British.

LEFT: **Aerial reconnaisance after the Fleet Air Arm attack on** *Taranto* **showed one Italian Cavour class battleship badly damaged, one beached with a heavy list to starboard and the other with her stern submerged and leaking oil.** ABOVE: **The Italian battleship** *Caio Duilio* **photographed on the morning after the attack, with the whole of her starboard side submerged.** BELOW: **The sad end for one of** *Illustrious*'s **Swordfish, recovered from the harbour after the attack on** *Taranto*. **Despite their frailty, the Swordfish could survive considerable damage.**

When Cunningham planned Operation Judgement in November 1941 – a complex passage of ships through the Mediterranean and an attack on the Italians in Taranto harbour – the Italians outnumbered Cunningham in every class of ship except carriers. *Malaya, Ramillies, Valiant* and *Warspite* formed the covering force, while torpedo-bombers from the carrier *Illustrious* sank or badly damaged *Vittorio Veneto, Caio Duilio* and *Conte di Cavour*. Japanese naval officers studied the results as they prepared for an attack on the US fleet at Pearl Harbor.

At the Battle of Cape Matapan in March 1941, the Italians sent the battleship *Vittorio Veneto* to interrupt British convoys south of Greece, and, again warned by intelligence, Cunningham sailed his ships. British cruisers retired eastwards towards Cunningham's battleships, hoping to draw the Italians into a trap, while the Italian Admiral Iachino hoped to catch them between his heavy cruisers and the *Vittorio Veneto*. However, aircraft from the carrier *Formidable* attacked the Italian battleship, and, without his own air cover, Iachino realized he must retreat westwards. *Vittorio Veneto* was hit once by torpedo, and the heavy cruiser *Pola* was stopped, also by a torpedo.

Iachino ordered ships to protect *Pola*, but shortly after ten o'clock that night, radar in the British battleships revealed their position. Immediately, *Barham, Valiant* and *Warspite* opened fire at close range sinking two Italian heavy cruisers, and in the night fighting which followed two Italian destroyers and *Pola* were sunk.

However, the end of the battleship age was marked in the Mediterranean by the dramatic sinking of the elderly *Barham*, which on November 25, 1941, with the battleships *Queen Elizabeth* and *Valiant* formed part of Force K hunting for Italian

convoys off North Africa. She was hit by three torpedoes from the German submarine *U-331*, quickly capsized and blew up with large loss of life.

Battleships played a supporting role in the Allied landings in North Africa and Sicily and in Italy. In November 1942 three US battleships covered the landings at Casablanca, whilst in the Mediterranean Force H covered the landings in Algeria. At Salerno in September 1943 the heavy guns of *Warspite* and *Valiant*, turned on targets ashore, played a major role in stopping a German counter-attack.

The surrender of the Italian fleet released the Royal Navy's capital ships for duties elsewhere and the war at sea in the Mediterranean was then mostly conducted by light ships. Nevertheless, during Operation Dragoon, the last major landings in the Mediterranean, in southern France, there were five battleships, one British, three American and a Frenchman, fighting for the liberty of France.

LEFT: **Pearl Harbor, December 7, 1941: a Japanese aerial picture that shows "battleship row" already under attack. A British officer who visited earlier and saw the Americans' lack of preparedness had noted "you can't miss".** ABOVE: **Admiral Isoroku Yamamoto, architect of the pre-emptive attack on Pearl Harbor, who realized that the only hope of defeating the USA was to wipe out its fleet. He might have succeeded but intelligence did not tell him that the USN carriers were not present.**

Nemesis at Pearl Harbor

When the British battleship *Warspite* visited Pearl Harbor in August 1941, one of her officers, a veteran of the Fleet Air Arm in the Mediterranean, saw battleship row and remarked, "Blimey, you can't miss!" The Imperial Japanese Navy (IJN) had followed events in the Mediterranean, particularly the attack on Taranto in which a handful of unsophisticated biplanes had crippled the Italian battle fleet.

The Washington Naval Treaty was aimed at preventing a naval arms race and forbade the building of naval bases closer to Japan than Singapore (UK) and the Philippines (USA). However, the Anglo-Japanese treaties were not renewed, and after the conquest of Manchuria in 1937, Japan invaded China. The USA aided China and imposed sanctions on Japan, eventually cutting off the supply of oil and raw materials. By 1940, Japan had aligned herself with Nazi Germany and was developing plans to occupy South-east Asia and seize the resources she needed. The Japanese army and navy were well versed in amphibious warfare and naval aviation, but the threat to Japanese plans was the US Navy (USN) fleet based at Pearl Harbor, Hawaii. Earlier in the century, the IJN had launched a pre-emptive strike on Port Arthur, and now Admiral Yamamoto devised a plan to annihilate the USN with a surprise attack.

The key element of Yamamoto's plan was the surprise use of aircraft carriers and naval aircraft on a scale never seen before. Training began in the spring of 1941, and the plan was approved in October. The carrier force commanded by Vice Admiral Chuichi Nagumo consisted of six heavy aircraft carriers and their escorts, and a submarine force was deployed to sink any American warships that escaped from Pearl Harbor. Nagumo's fleet assembled in a remote anchorage in the Kurile Islands and crossed the northern Pacific unobserved. By dawn on Sunday December 7, 1941, the Nagumo fleet was some 320km/200 miles north of Hawaii.

At 06.00, the first wave of 181 planes composed of torpedo bombers, dive-bombers and fighters attacked the USN's Pacific Fleet at its anchorage and achieved complete surprise. There were more than 90 ships at anchor in Pearl Harbor, including eight battleships, seven in a row off Ford Island, and the *Pennsylvania* in dry dock close by. Within minutes of the first attack, all had been bombed and torpedoed. *West Virginia* sank quickly; *Oklahoma* turned turtle; a fire in *Arizona* ignited the forward magazine and she blew up; *California, Maryland, Tennessee, Pennsylvania,* and *Nevada* were also damaged.

Half an hour later, a second wave of 170 Japanese planes made a concentrated attack on *Nevada*, which despite damage got underway. However, *Nevada* had to be beached to keep the channel clear. The Japanese attack on Pearl Harbor ended shortly before 10.00 am, by which time 21 USN ships were sunk or damaged including, in addition to the battleships, three cruisers, four destroyers, a seaplane tender, the former battleship *Utah* (converted to a target), a repair ship, a minelayer, a tug and a floating dock. The Japanese had also

ABOVE: *Nevada* was the only USN battleship to get underway during the attack and is seen here moving away from other burning ships. Her ensign is still in the harbour position. RIGHT: The battleships *West Virginia* and *Tennessee* still upright but burning fiercely after the attack was over. Both ships were later repaired and fought in the Pacific theatre. BELOW RIGHT: *Arizona* was not to be so lucky. After a raging fire reached her forward magazine, she blew up. The US President called it "a day of infamy", and the effect of the attack was to shock and mobilize the American people and especially the USN. It was inevitable that the USA with its superior industrial might would eventually prevail over Japan.

struck at the airfields of Hawaii, where over 188 US aircraft were destroyed and 159 damaged, mostly on the ground.

Japanese losses were less than 10 per cent of the attacking aircraft, yet the attack on Pearl Harbor was not as successful as it might have been. By chance, there were no USN aircraft carriers in harbour. The carriers *Enterprise* and *Lexington* were at sea delivering aircraft reinforcements to other American Pacific bases and *Saratoga*, which might also have been present, was in refit on the West Coast. Damage to the harbour installations was slight, and these were quickly brought back into full use, and all but three ships sunk or damaged at Pearl Harbor were salvaged. Of the battleships, *Arizona* was too badly damaged to be raised, *Oklahoma* was raised but considered too old to be worth repair, and *Utah* was already considered obsolete.

President Roosevelt called the attack on Pearl Harbor "a day of infamy", while the blow to American prestige and anger at the sudden and unexpected strike precipitated the USA into World War II, with the USA declaring war on Germany as well as Japan.

Hunt for the *Bismarck*

Following the success of Operation Berlin in which the battleships *Scharnhorst* and *Gneisenau* had sunk 22 allied merchant ships during a two-month raid into the Atlantic, a new operation was planned. Operation Rheinübung would use Germany's newest and most powerful battleship, *Bismarck*. Originally, it was intended that *Scharnhorst* and *Gneisenau* would sail from Brest too, but neither was operational after being bombed. Consideration was also given to delaying the operation until *Tirpitz* was worked up, but the German leadership could not wait and the heavy cruiser *Prinz Eugen* was selected as *Bismarck*'s consort. The supporting force consisted of two supply ships, five tankers and two scouting ships despatched secretly into the Atlantic.

However, both warships were seen heading north off the Swedish coast and Fleet Air Arm reconnaissance confirmed that they had sailed from Bergen. *Bismarck* and the cruiser *Prinz Eugen* were next detected in the Denmark Strait late on May 23, by the watching British heavy cruisers *Suffolk* and *Norfolk*, who shadowed until the morning of May 24, 1940, when the battlecruiser *Hood* and the new battleship *Prince of Wales* came into action.

At 05.32, *Hood* opened fire on *Prinz Eugen* at 21km/13 miles range, and both German ships replied, firing at *Hood*. A fire started on *Hood*'s upper deck and at about 06.00 the *Bismarck*'s fifth salvo hit and *Hood* blew up. The German fire now shifted to *Prince of Wales*, hitting several times and killing or wounding everyone on the bridge except the captain. However, *Bismarck* had been hit with two or three 355mm/14in shells before breaking off the action.

Although *Bismarck* was losing fuel and shipping water, the German admiral, Lütjens, decided to continue his North Atlantic sortie. With one boiler room out of action and speed reduced to 28 knots, he first feinted north while ordering *Prinz Eugen* to proceed independently, and then resumed a course towards western France.

TOP LEFT: **This stern view of the German battleship *Bismarck* gives some idea of the strength and size of the German monster. Nevertheless, though she sank the British *Hood*, her career was measured in months.** ABOVE: **Battle at sea between battleships took place at long range and often all either side saw of the enemy was distant smoke on the horizon.**

Around midnight Fleet Air Arm Swordfish torpedo bombers from the carrier *Victorious* found *Bismarck*, launched their torpedoes and hit her amidships on the armoured belt, with no apparent effect. Then during the night, *Bismarck* shook off *Norfolk* and *Suffolk*, which had been keeping contact by radar. Lütjens now had a chance to escape but, assuming that he was still being shadowed by radar, he thought that nothing would be lost by a long signal to Germany that gave away his position.

After 30 hours without a sighting, a Catalina flying-boat of the RAF, flown by a USN officer, Ensign Smith, spotted *Bismarck* on May 26. He held contact under fire while radioing *Bismarck*'s position and the cruiser *Sheffield* was able to resume shadowing.

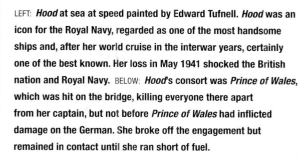

LEFT: *Hood* at sea at speed painted by Edward Tufnell. *Hood* was an icon for the Royal Navy, regarded as one of the most handsome ships and, after her world cruise in the interwar years, certainly one of the best known. Her loss in May 1941 shocked the British nation and Royal Navy. BELOW: *Hood*'s consort was *Prince of Wales*, which was hit on the bridge, killing everyone there apart from her captain, but not before *Prince of Wales* had inflicted damage on the German. She broke off the engagement but remained in contact until she ran short of fuel.

ABOVE: **In the final stage of the battle, *Rodney* closed to a few thousand metres/yards to pulverize *Bismarck* at the modern equivalent of point blank range while the battleship *King George V* stood off and hit *Bismarck* with plunging fire.**

Meanwhile the Royal Navy was gathering in the Atlantic. On May 22, Admiral Tovey with the capital ships *King George V* and *Repulse* and the carrier *Victorious* had steamed west and south from Scapa Flow. *Rodney* and *Ramillies* had left their convoys and were steaming south-west and Captain Vian with the Fourth Destroyer Flotilla had left a troop convoy to sail east. *Bismarck*, although more than 600 miles from France, might yet reach safety before the Royal Navy could catch up.

However, Force H, consisting of the battlecruiser *Renown* and carrier *Ark Royal* were approaching from Gibraltar. A torpedo strike by Swordfish biplanes on the afternoon of May 26 found the shadowing *Sheffield* in error. As darkness fell, a second strike found its target but cloud offered little protection against *Bismarck*'s radar laid guns, and as the Swordfish converged from different bearings, *Bismarck* used her heavy

guns to raise walls of water against the frail aircraft. Many aircraft were damaged but none were lost and two torpedoes hit their target, jamming the rudders and dooming *Bismarck*. As engineers tried to free her steering, *Bismarck* steered north towards the British, while Captain Vian and his destroyers, including the Polish *Piorun*, made a series of torpedo attacks.

At 08.45 on May 27, Tovey's heavy ships caught up and opened fire. At first, *Bismarck*'s reply was accurate but she quickly became a wreck as *Rodney*'s 405mm/16in guns found the enemy range. *Rodney* closed to 3,650m/4,000 yards to fire at point blank range while *King George V*'s fire from 12,800m/14,000 yards plunged down on *Bismarck*, and, within 30 minutes, coordinated resistance had ceased. The fire-control positions were out of action, communications to the engine rooms and compartments below the armoured deck had been lost, and fires raged. A myth would grow up that *Bismarck*'s crew scuttled her, but between 10.15 and 10.35, the cruiser *Dorsetshire* torpedoed *Bismarck* from port and starboard, finally causing *Bismarck* to heel over and sink in five minutes. Only 115 men survived from a crew of more than 2,000.

Battleship versus battleship in the Pacific

LEFT: The modern *Washington* photographed off New York in August 1942. Her encounter with the elderly Japanese *Kirishima* in November was the last battleship-to-battleship engagement. BELOW: *Kirishima,* built as a battlecruiser, had been modernized with new guns and new armour in the interwar years and the Japanese navy rated her as a battleship. She is seen here in Sukumo Bay, 1937. The cut-away forecastle discloses her World War I origins and the upright funnels suggest a British provenance to her design.

The last great battle involving battleships would not be until the Battle of Leyte Gulf in October 1944, but by then battleships were ancillary to aircraft carriers and naval aircraft. However, the last battle in which battleship fought battleship in the Pacific was during the epic months-long struggle between the Japanese and the Americans over Guadalcanal in the Solomon Islands. The Japanese hoped to turn the Solomons into a base to cut off Australia, and in 1942 started to build airfields along the chain of islands. In turn, the Americans wanted to use Guadalcanal as their base of operations against the Japanese further north.

The first Battle of Savo took place on 12/13 November as the Japanese tried to reinforce their troops on the island and to bombard Henderson airfield: the Japanese force was centred on the battleships *Hiei* and *Kirishima*. The ensuing battle by night and in heavy rain was disorganized and both sides suffered as their formations passed through each other. The American cruisers and destroyers suffered more but the Japanese battleship *Hiei* sank next day.

Two nights later, on November 14/15, the Japanese *Kirishima*, the heavy cruisers *Atago* and *Takao*, the light cruisers *Nagara* and *Sendai*, and nine destroyers tried to bombard Henderson Field again.

Although *Kirishima* was constructed as a battlecruiser and completed in 1915, she had twice been modernized, in 1927–30 and 1935–6: her armour was improved, she was lengthened and had modern machinery installed. Armed with eight 355mm/14in guns, the Japanese rated her as a battleship.

She had received light damage during a night action off Guadalcanal on November 12/13, when she met the Americans again. Her opponents this time were the two new battleships *Washington* and *South Dakota*, both completed within the last few months and armed with nine 405mm/16in guns, and their escort of four destroyers.

The Americans were in line ahead, in the order: four destroyers, *Washington* and *South Dakota* as they made a sweep north between Russell and Guadalcanal, then east and south-east, passing north of Savo. At about midnight contacts were seen on radar to the east, and *Sendai* and a destroyer immediately came under heavy fire. A few minutes later *Nagara* and the Japanese destroyers engaged the American destroyers, sinking three and damaging the fourth.

However, *South Dakota* had been illuminated and came under particularly heavy gun and torpedo attack. None of the 30 torpedoes hit her but she was hit several times by shellfire and lost electrical supply to her radar. According to the American admiral's official report, "What appeared to be the South Dakota was seen at about 01.21 at a considerable distance to the south-eastward between this ship and Guadalcanal on a southerly course".

Meanwhile *Washington*, which had not been engaged by the Japanese, succeeded in closing the range. From 00.16 to 00.19 *Washington* fired 42 405mm//16in rounds and her gunnery was highly effective. Fire opened at 17,000m/ 18,500yd range and hits were obtained by the third salvo.

She opened fire again between 01.00 and 01.07 after the target had been tracked by radar. The range was 7,700m/8,400yd and a hit was probably obtained on the first salvo and certainly on the second. *Kirishima* was hit nine times and burst into flames. Her return fire ceased and she was seen on radar to perform a 500-degree turn and draw off to the north-east.

The last major Japanese naval thrust at Guadalcanal had been turned back. *Washington* had done what she had been designed for and defeated one of her kind. In fact, *Washington* was the only American battleship to defeat another battleship. All the other battleship duels between the USN and the Imperial Japanese Navy involved ship- or land-based aircraft.

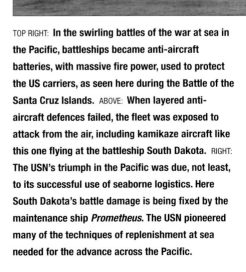

TOP RIGHT: **In the swirling battles of the war at sea in the Pacific, battleships became anti-aircraft batteries, with massive fire power, used to protect the US carriers, as seen here during the Battle of the Santa Cruz Islands.** ABOVE: **When layered anti-aircraft defences failed, the fleet was exposed to attack from the air, including kamikaze aircraft like this one flying at the battleship South Dakota.** RIGHT: **The USN's triumph in the Pacific was due, not least, to its successful use of seaborne logistics. Here South Dakota's battle damage is being fixed by the maintenance ship *Prometheus*. The USN pioneered many of the techniques of replenishment at sea needed for the advance across the Pacific.**

Battleship war in the Pacific

During World War II, the conflict in the east was primarily a naval war. After the Japanese attack on Pearl Harbor and the sinking of *Repulse* and *Prince of Wales* on December 10, 1941, the Japanese enjoyed an unbroken series of victories. Their aim was to occupy the American bases at Guam and Wake, capture the Philippines, seize Burma, Malaya, Singapore, and the Dutch East Indies, and then to fortify a ring of islands in the south and the central Pacific. The plan seemed to be successful and by early 1942 the Japanese had conquered an empire.

However, Japanese expansion reached its high-water mark in March 1942. The US Navy (USN) had been studying its strategy for a war in the Pacific for many years. The result was Plan Orange, which envisaged a campaign stretching across the Pacific Ocean and culminating in a decisive battle with the Imperial Japanese Navy (IJN). Accordingly, Admiral Nimitz began his counter-attack and in May 1942 the Japanese advance was stopped at the Battle of the Coral Sea. A month later, the Japanese suffered a major defeat at the Battle of Midway in the central Pacific. In August 1942, US Marines landed on Guadalcanal, beginning a month-long battle for possession. USN carrier-borne aircraft had supported the landings, but when the carriers withdrew the Japanese were able to counter-attack, and at the Battle of Savo Island, the Japanese navy sank four heavy cruisers, including the Australian *Canberra*, and one destroyer. Neither side could establish clear naval nor air superiority and the success of the campaign swung in the balance: Guadalcanal became a battle of attrition and in such a campaign the Americans were bound eventually to win.

The USN's strategy required resources and it required the development of the tactics and techniques of amphibious warfare and naval air power. Battleships were to play an

ABOVE: **Three ships from the South Dakota class were present at the Battle of Leyte Gulf: *South Dakota*, *Massachusetts* and *Alabama*. Here one of them fires a broadside from her main batteries.** LEFT: **Admiral Chester W Nimitz, the USN Commander-in-Chief Pacific during World War II, who led the US naval offensive, first from the Solomon Islands in 1942 to the north and west, and then, in 1944, to the coasts of the Japanese islands.**

ancillary role, bombarding enemy positions ashore and providing anti-aircraft defence for the fleet: as the war developed, USN battleships were massively rearmed with light guns. In November 1943, American industrial might was able to provide Nimitz with the strength he needed for an island-hopping campaign, and when US Marines met stubborn resistance and learned costly lessons, Nimitz opted to avoid strongly held islands and strike at the enemy's weakest points.

In 1944 and 1945 these hops developed into leaps as two amphibious offensives developed, American General MacArthur advancing via New Guinea into the Philippines and Nimitz reaching 3,200km/2,000 miles across the ocean from the Gilbert Islands to Okinawa. It was clear that while the Americans could replace their resources, the Japanese could not. At the Battle of the Philippine Sea in what USN pilots called "the great Marianas turkey shoot", Japanese naval air power was destroyed.

In October 1944, the Japanese navy planned to use their last carriers, including two hybrid conversions from battleships, *Ise* and *Hyuga*, to decoy American forces away from the beachheads of Leyte Gulf to enable their battleships to bombard them and to destroy the shipping offshore. The plan almost succeeded, with two battleship forces planned to converge on the invasion beaches. A southern force consisted of the battleships *Fuso* and *Yamashiro*, while a central force contained the five battleships *Yamato, Musashi, Nagato, Kongo* and *Haruna*. Opposing them were the six USN battleships *Iowa, New Jersey, Massachusetts, South Dakota,*

Washington, and *Alabama*: however, the USN fleet also contained 32 aircraft carriers and over 1,700 aircraft with experienced pilots, whereas the Japanese could only muster three carriers and fewer than 200 planes. The battle raged over several hundred miles of sea and although the Japanese reached the invasion beaches, they did not press home their attack. At the end of the Battle of Leyte Gulf, the Imperial Japanese Navy had effectively ceased to exist.

Japanese resistance did not end with the destruction of their fleet and in April 1945 off Okinawa, the Japanese launched large-scale suicide raids resulting in 26 Allied warships being sunk and many more damaged. A date had been set for the invasion of Japan when atomic bombs were dropped on Hiroshima and Nagasaki on August 6 and 9, 1945, and in Tokyo Bay on September 2, 1945, the battleship *Missouri* provided a theatrical background for the signing of the Japanese surrender. Also present were the American battleships *Colorado, Mississippi, Idaho, New Mexico, Iowa, South Dakota* and *West Virginia*, and the British battleships *King George V* and *Duke of York*.

The USA emerged from the war with global commitments and the largest navy the world had ever seen, but the age of the battleship was almost over.

ABOVE LEFT: **Many lonely beaches became battlegrounds, such as this beach in Leyte Gulf where Japanese shipping was bombed and strafed from the air by the advancing Allies' naval aircraft.** LEFT: **By 1945 nowhere was safe for Japanese battleships, not even their own home port of Kure, seen here under high level attack by the USAF.** ABOVE: **As Japanese air power waned, the Japanese resorted to kamikaze or suicide attacks, in which young inexperienced pilots tried to crash their aircraft into Allied ships. The damage caused – seen here in the Australian cruiser *Australia* – could be severe.**

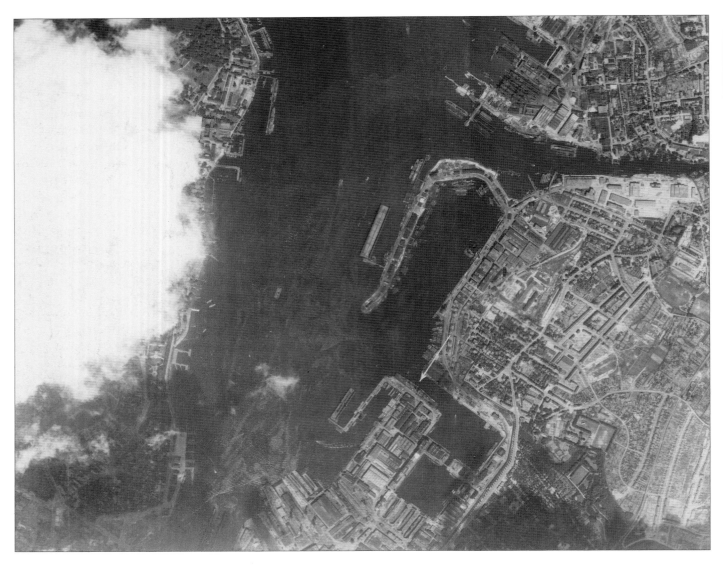

The German navy in World War II

In 1933–6 the revived German navy completed building the pocket battleships *Deutschland, Admiral Scheer* and *Admiral Graf Spee*. In 1935 the Anglo-German Naval Agreement was concluded, which allowed the Germans to build up to 35 per cent of the British warship tonnage. The Germans also drew up a secret "Plan Z" which by 1945 would give their navy six battleships, four pocket battleships and four battlecruisers in addition to the four battleships and three pocket battleships already in existence. However the outbreak of hostilities was to intervene well before this plan could be fulfilled.

In August 1939 two German pocket battleships, their supply ships and a force of U-boats were deployed into the Atlantic. On September 30, *Admiral Graf Spee* sank her first ship, and seven British and French hunting groups including three battleships were formed to hunt her down. After a brief sortie in November into the Indian Ocean, *Admiral Graf Spee* returned to the South Atlantic. On December 13 she met Force G, consisting of one heavy and two light cruisers, and was driven into Montevideo and scuttled.

ABOVE: **Through the cloud, aerial reconnaissance of Kiel, the German navy's base at the eastern or Baltic end of the Kiel canal, shows *Scharnhorst* alongside and vulnerable to attack.**

Meanwhile her sister ship *Deutschland* sank two ships in the North Atlantic and was ordered home where Hitler, fearing a loss of prestige should she be damaged or sunk under the name of the fatherland, had her renamed *Lützow*.

In early October *Gneisenau* sortied off Norway in a repeat of World War I tactics, to draw British ships within range of German U-boats and aircraft. *Hood, Nelson, Repulse, Rodney* and *Royal Oak* all sailed but did not make contact.

On November 23 *Scharnhorst* and *Gneisenau*, while attempting a breakout into the Atlantic, sank the armed merchant cruiser *Rawalpindi* but returned to Germany to avoid the searching British ships.

During the Norway Campaign in spring 1940 the battlecruisers *Scharnhorst* and *Gneisenau* covered the northern landings, and were briefly engaged by the British *Renown*, with

LEFT: *Scharnhorst* and *Gneisenau* were blockaded in western France for many months, but in February 1942 made a daring dash up the English Channel. Their escape was a tactical defeat for the Royal Navy but a strategic blunder for the Germans.

mutual, slight damage. The Germans escaped in a snowstorm and there were to be no other battleship-to-battleship engagements. However *Scharnhorst* was hit by a torpedo from the destroyer *Acasta* and again on June 13 by aircraft from *Ark Royal*. On June 20 *Gneisenau* was torpedoed by the submarine *Clyde*, blowing a huge hole in her bows. As a result both ships were out of action until the end of the year.

Between October 1940 and March 1941 *Admiral Scheer* raided in the Atlantic and Indian Oceans, sinking 16 ships of 100,650 tonnes/99,059 tons, including the armed merchant cruiser *Jervis Bay* and five ships of convoy HX84. The disruption to convoys across the Atlantic had a very serious effect on Britain, and diverted battleships to convoy protection. On February 8, 1941, *Scharnhorst* and *Gneisenau* found convoy HX106 escorted by *Ramillies* but declined to attack and *Ramillies* was too slow to catch them up. In March *Scharnhorst* and *Gneisenau* were sighted by aircraft from *Malaya* escorting convoy SL67 but again they escaped, finally taking refuge in Brest having sunk 22 merchant ships.

The hunt for the *Bismarck* is told separately, but her loss marked the end of independent raiding by German surface warships in the Atlantic, and when in June *Lützow* attempted a breakout she was torpedoed and forced to return to Germany.

The ships at Brest suffered repeated bomber attacks, and on February 11–13, 1942, they made a daring escape. The Channel Dash of *Scharnhorst, Gneisenau* and the cruiser *Prinz Eugen* was an embarrassment and a tactical defeat, but also a strategic gain for the Royal Navy. The Brest Squadron ceased to be a threat to convoys, the heavy ships were damaged by mines and two weeks later *Gneisenau* was so badly bombed at Kiel that she never went to sea again.

TOP RIGHT: **At the end of the Norway Campaign in the spring of 1940, during the invasion and counter-invasion of Norway by Germany and by Britain and her allies, the British carrier *Glorious* was caught and sunk by the German navy on June 8. Here the German warship *Scharnhorst* fires on the carrier.** RIGHT: **The German warships *Scharnhorst*, *Gneisenau* and *Hipper* at anchor in a Norwegian fjord in 1940.**

Thereafter the concentration of German ships in Norwegian waters dominated Royal Navy strategy in the north. The convoys had to be given strong escorts, including ships such as the battleships *Duke of York*, *Renown* and *King George V*, together with aircraft carriers.

Between March 6 and 9, 1942, *Tirpitz* was hunted by the British Home Fleet but when she was located, aircraft from the carrier *Victorious* failed to press home the attack. However *Tirpitz* never put to sea again. The story of convoy PQ17 and the Battles of the Barents Sea and of North Cape in 1942 and 1943 is also told separately.

Tirpitz was finally destroyed by RAF action in November 1944. In March 1945 *Gneisenau* was sunk as a block ship at Gdynia, in April *Admiral Scheer* was bombed and capsized, and shortly before Germany surrendered on 8 May, *Lützow*, the last of the German battleships, was scuttled.

Convoy PQ17 and the Battles of the Barents Sea and the North Cape

Hitler became obsessed with the idea that the British would invade Norway, and he wanted his heavy ships stationed there, where they were also a threat to the Arctic convoys which the Allies were pushing through to Russia. By July 1942 the threatening German ships consisted of *Tirpitz*, *Lützow*, *Admiral Scheer* and others. So when convoy PQ17 of 36 ships left Iceland on June 27 the escort consisted of American and British cruisers and destroyers, and the covering force contained the British *Duke of York* and carrier *Victorious*, and the USN battleship *Washington*. When on July 3 a false appreciation of intelligence led the Admiralty in London to withdraw the escort and concentrate the fleet against a reported movement by *Tirpitz*, there was a massacre of the convoy by U-boats and aircraft. Only 11 ships eventually reached Archangel over the next few days and weeks. In fact *Tirpitz*'s sortie was half-hearted, but the threat was sufficient to denude the convoy of its escort and halt Arctic convoys for the next three months.

In December 1942 convoy JW51B of 14 ships sailed from Scotland for Russia escorted by destroyers under the command of Captain Rupert Sherbrooke in *Onslow*, and covered by the cruisers *Jamaica* and *Sheffield*. Opposing the convoy were *Tirpitz* and *Lützow*, the cruisers *Admiral Hipper*, *Köln* and *Nürnberg*, and several destroyers. This long series of quickly changing and confused actions became known as the Battle of the Barents Sea.

As the convoy passed south of Bear Island in the darkness and snow, *Lützow*, *Hipper* and six destroyers put to sea to intercept it, and, on the morning of New Year's Eve, *Hipper* and three destroyers attacked the convoy from the north, driving it towards *Lützow* in the south. *Hipper* first fired on the destroyer *Obdurate*, but her approach to the convoy was thwarted by the destroyers *Onslow*, *Orwell* and *Obedient*, although Sherbrooke (who was subsequently awarded the VC) was badly wounded.

TOP: **Throughout World War II the German navy used the Norwegian fjords to try and outflank the Royal Navy and as bases for sorties into the Atlantic, or to attack Russian conveys. Here *Admiral Hipper*, *Admiral Scheer* and escorts leave for an operation.** ABOVE: **Threat of German capital ships to the Russian convoy caused the allies much anxiety, and in July 1942, after convoy PQ17 had been ordered to scatter, the route was abandoned until the days grew shorter.**

TOP LEFT: **A World War I picture of Admiral Franz von Hipper, who led the German battlecruisers at the Battle of Jutland in 1916.** ABOVE: **The Germans tried to hide their ships using camouflage and smokescreens when attacked.** LEFT: **The heavy cruiser *Hipper,* shown here at anchor in a Norwegian fjord, was part of the forces that threatened allied convoys.** BELOW: **Admiral Sir Bruce Fraser, photographed in January 1944 on the quarterdeck of *Duke of York* with his band of brothers, after the last-ever action between capital ships in home waters.**

Hipper sank a minesweeper and damaged the destroyer *Achates*, but when the British cruisers announced their arrival with accurate radar-laid gunfire *Hipper* was damaged and an escorting destroyer, *Friedrich Eckoldt*, was sunk. *Hipper* still tried to get into the convoy but the destroyers skilfully used smoke and the threat of torpedoes to keep her out.

Meanwhile *Lützow* approached from the south but was timidly managed and driven off by the remaining British destroyers: by noon of a very short midwinter's day both German ships were withdrawing, chased by their smaller opponents. The convoy reached Kola without loss whilst *Hipper* never saw action again, and *Lützow*'s intended breakout into the Atlantic was thwarted. When Hitler learned that the heavy German units had been driven off by light cruisers and destroyers, he raged, calling the heavy ships a waste of resources and ordering them to be paid off. The order was rescinded but Grand Admiral Raeder resigned.

Nearly one year later, on December 20, 1943, convoy JW55B consisting of 19 ships sailed for Russia covered by *Duke of York* and the cruiser *Jamaica*, while the return convoy RA55A sailed from Kola on December 23 protected by the cruisers *Belfast*, *Norfolk* and *Sheffield*. On Christmas Day *Scharnhorst* and five destroyers sailed to intercept. As convoy JW55B passed south of Bear Island in stormy weather, *Scharnhorst*'s approach was detected on radar and she was fired on and hit by the cruiser *Norfolk*. As *Scharnhorst* tried to

work to the north round the convoy, she was again engaged by the British cruisers and hit, although *Norfolk* was in turn badly damaged by 280mm/11in shells.

Scharnhorst then turned south away from the convoy but she was shadowed on radar, and her position reported to *Duke of York*, who was in an ideal position to the south-west to cut off her retreat. In a coordinated attack the cruisers fired starshells and attacked from one side of *Scharnhorst* while *Duke of York*, with the cruiser *Jamaica* close astern to confuse German radar, attacked from the other. The British battleship's 355mm/14in guns soon found their range and *Scharnhorst* was quickly silenced and finished off by some 10 or 11 torpedoes, sinking with huge loss of life.

The Battle of the North Cape was the last battleship-on-battleship action that took place between the Royal Navy and the German navy.

The battleship after World War II

By the end of World War II it was obvious to all naval strategists that the aircraft carrier, with its long-range offensive power and air defence capabilities, would be the capital ship of the future. Furthermore, in the absence of air cover, the battleship had been shown to be extremely vulnerable to air attack.

Once hostilities had ceased, the Royal Navy was quick to dispose of its battleships, with the majority being broken up by 1949. Of the remaining ships, *Anson* was broken up in 1957 after a period in reserve, and the *Duke of York* was scrapped in 1958. *Vanguard*, the last battleship to be completed for the Royal Navy, was commissioned too late to see service in World War II, and served as a training ship before being placed in reserve in 1956 and broken up in 1960.

France continued to operate her two battleships *Richelieu* and *Jean Bart* for a number of years after the war. *Richelieu* was deployed for fire support duties during French operations in Indo-China in 1945–46, then placed in reserve in 1956 and broken up in 1960. *Jean Bart* operated during the Suez campaign in 1956, providing fire support for the ground forces and anti-aircraft cover for the Anglo-French fleet. She operated as a gunnery training vessel until 1969, when she was finally scrapped.

The Italian battleship fleet was also quickly reduced following the end of World War II. Of those that survived, *Andrea Doria* was used as a training ship until 1956 and broken up in 1961, and *Giulio Cesare* was transferred to the Soviet Navy as the *Novorossiysk* under the terms of the peace treaty in 1948. She later blew up and sank in Sevastopol harbour in 1955.

ABOVE: **The spectacle of *Iowa* firing her main ordnance.** BELOW: ***Wisconsin* seen here with a considerable battery of secondary and tertiary armament. Much of this was replaced by missile technology in later refits.**

The US battleship fleet also underwent drastic reductions at the end of the war, with many vessels being decommissioned and scrapped. However, a number of these historic ships escaped the breaker's yard and are now preserved as museum ships in the United States. *Arkansas*, *New York*, *Nevada* and *Pennsylvania* were not so lucky, and they were assigned to the atom bomb testing programme at Bikini Atoll

ABOVE: **The Italian battleship *Giulio Cesare* was allocated as reparations to the Soviets in 1948, becoming the ill-fated *Novorossiysk*.** RIGHT: **Three of the *Iowa*-class battleships in 1967: *Wisconsin*, *New Jersey* and *Iowa*.**

in the Marshall Islands. *Arkansas* was destroyed during the second nuclear detonation, but the remaining three hulls survived to be sunk as target ships off Hawaii and Kwajalein by conventional munitions. The only Japanese battleship to survive the war, *Nagato*, was also expended during the US nuclear testing programme.

American battleships of the Iowa class were perhaps most fortunate as they continued to serve intermittently until the early 1990s. Reactivated in 1950–51 for the Korean War, their electronics were updated and aircraft and launch catapults were removed. All of the smaller anti-aircraft automatic weapons were also removed since these were useless against modern jet-propelled aircraft. In addition, all ships of the class except *Missouri* were equipped to handle a 406mm/16in nuclear shell, for which a dedicated magazine was constructed and special handling arrangements were developed. Following the cease-fire, all four ships went back into reserve. In 1968 the *New Jersey* was taken out of reserve and given a very rapid, basic overhaul so that she could be deployed off the coast of Vietnam in a fire support role.

In the early 1980s the four Iowas were overhauled again, this time receiving extensive modernization. Quadruple missile launchers were installed for 32 Tomahawk cruise missiles and 16 Harpoon anti-shipping missiles. Four of the redundant 127mm/5in gun mountings were removed and four Vulcan-Phalanx close-in weapon systems (CIWS) were installed to provide close proximity protection. New electronics were also installed and these in turn required the fitting of a new mast arrangement. Restrictions were also placed on the firing arcs of the main ordnance as blast effects could badly damage the sensitive new electronics and missile systems.

In 1991, *Wisconsin* and *Missouri* were sent to support the Coalition forces in the Persian Gulf during operation Desert Storm. *Wisconsin* operated from the waters of the Red Sea during the opening phases of the campaign, while *Missouri* sailed into the Gulf to join other Coalition warships. Together they launched more than 50 Tomahawk cruise missiles at ranges of up to 1,287km/800 miles, and *Missouri* also shelled Iraqi positions in Kuwait. On their return to the United States, these two warships were taken out of commission, bringing to an end the era of the battleship.

Where are they now?

Apart from a number of beautifully preserved US battleships, the only remaining examples of these mighty vessels are those that were sunk in action and still lie submerged in their final resting place beneath the waves. Regrettably, the European nations chose to decommission their remaining capital ships shortly after the end of World War II to reduce the huge associated overheads. Once out of commission, the vessels were quickly scrapped, with only a few parts being preserved for display in museums.

Since the 1980s, there has been a resurgence of interest in locating the wrecks of many of the capital ships lost in World War II. This has coincided with technological developments that have enabled deep sea sonar scanning to identify possible wreck sites, and the use of small submersibles and remotely operated underwater vehicles (ROVs) equipped with specially developed cameras to investigate and record what is found.

The *Royal Oak* rests in 30m/98ft of water at Scapa Flow where she sank in 1939. Her ship's bell was salvaged and placed as a memorial at Kirkwall Cathedral. Despite the shallow depth of the water, the wreck is an official war grave and remains off-limit to divers.

Two ships of the Royal Sovereign class, *Resolution* and *Ramillies*, each have a single 381mm/15in gun displayed on a concrete mount in front of the Imperial War Museum in London.

In 2001, the wreck of HMS *Hood* was discovered with the use of sophisticated underwater sonar and ROVs. She lies in 2,800m/9,186ft of water below the Denmark Strait, where she sank with the loss of 1,415 men. The vessel is in poor condition, with the bow missing and the forward part of the ship upside down resting on its deck.

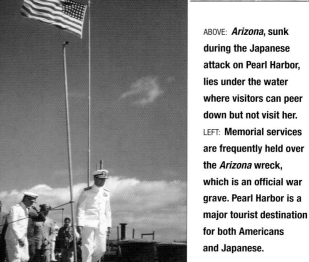

ABOVE: *Arizona*, sunk during the Japanese attack on Pearl Harbor, lies under the water where visitors can peer down but not visit her. LEFT: Memorial services are frequently held over the *Arizona* wreck, which is an official war grave. Pearl Harbor is a major tourist destination for both Americans and Japanese.

The *King George V*-class battleship *Prince of Wales* came to rest almost completely upside down in 70m/230ft of water, with one side of the main deck a few metres off the sandy bottom. Lying in clear, warm water, the torpedo damage to the hull is clearly visible. Like her companion *Repulse*, *Prince of Wales* "flies" a white ensign from one screw.

The World War I United States Navy battleship *Texas* is preserved at Houston, Texas, although she is displayed in the blue camouflage colour scheme and state of modernization which she was given in World War II. Other preserved USN battleships from World War II include *North Carolina* at Wilmington, *Massachusetts* at Fall River, *Alabama* at Mobile, *Iowa* at Suisun Bay, *New Jersey* at Camden, *Missouri* at Pearl Harbor, and *Wisconsin* at Norfolk. *Arizona* and *Utah* lie submerged at Pearl Harbor, where they are designated as war graves in memory of those lost in the Japanese attack.

Remains of the great Japanese battleship *Yamato* were found in 1985. She now lies in 305m/1,000ft of water with her bow section separated from the main hull.

The Japanese battleship *Nagato* was sunk at Bikini Atoll and now lies upside down on the bottom of the lagoon at a depth of 55m/180ft in clear, warm water, where she is reckoned to be the best battleship dive in the world.

The *Deutschland*-class pocket battleship *Admiral Graf Spee* lies exactly where she sank in 1939. She rests in 20m/65ft of murky water inside the Rio de la Plata about 5km/3 miles from Montevideo, Uruguay. In 1997, one of the *Graf Spee*'s guns was removed and restored, and now rests in front of Montevideo's National Maritime Museum. Further salvage operations have recovered the ship's range-finding equipment and a 1.8m/6ft bronze eagle.

In 2000, the submerged wreck of *Scharnhorst* was located 130km/65 miles north-northeast of North Cape at a depth 290m/950ft, and was later filmed with the use of an ROV. The wreck of *Scharnhorst* rests upside down on the sea bed and shows evidence of the heavy damage sustained during her final engagement in 1943.

Bismarck's remains were finally located in 1989. The wreck lies 966km/600 miles west of Brest at a depth of 4,790m/15,700ft in the Atlantic. Although heavily damaged by shell and torpedo impact, the wreck is in good condition, with the hull intact except for the last 10.7m/35ft of the stern that broke away. The main gun turrets separated from the hull under their own weight as the ship rolled over and sank, and they now lie upside down on the bottom.

Finally, the mighty German battleship *Tirpitz* was broken up in the 1950s in the Norwegian fjord where she was eventually sunk, but large parts of the ship still litter the seabed.

ABOVE LEFT: **A piece of armour plate from the wreck of the Japanese *Yamato*.** ABOVE: **Two of *Yamato*'s shells. The cars in the background give some idea of their size. The massive scale of the armour and armament were no proof against bombs and torpedoes from naval aircraft.** BELOW: **Attempts being made to lift *Utah*, which was still leaking oil as late as 1944. Eventually, the decision was made to leave her as a war grave.**

Directory of Battleships

The battleship, which had benefited from every kind of advance in technology in the 19th century, was threatened in the next century by two new weapons: the submarine and the aeroplane. The oldest and most powerful navy in the world, the Royal Navy, realized this and at the start of World War I had not only the largest fleet of battleships but also the largest fleet of modern submarines. The Royal Navy was also the first to experiment with taking aircraft to sea and by 1918 the Royal Naval Air Service was one of the largest air forces in the world. Even as these new weapons increased in numbers and effectiveness, the battleship held sway up to the beginning of World War II. Throughout the war there were sporadic clashes between British and Italian, British and German, and American and Japanese capital ships. However tactics and operations involving aircraft evolved so rapidly that by 1942 the aircraft carrier rather than the battleship was regarded as the new capital ship of the fleet. By the end of World War II such battleships as remained were not being replaced, though a few lingered on in active service with the USN.

LEFT: **American battleships in line ahead in the 1940s – still the optimum formation for bringing the maximum number of guns to bear upon an enemy, whatever technical changes had taken place over the previous century.**

Hood

When commissioned in 1920 *Hood* was the largest warship in the world, and between the wars she became an icon not just for the Royal Navy, but for the British Empire. *Hood* was generally regarded, in respect of the combination of fighting power, speed and protection, to be the most powerful ship in the world. She was also thought to be one of the most beautiful. During a ten-month world cruise in 1923–4 *Hood*, with the battlecruiser *Repulse* and their escorts, visited the British dominions and crossed the Pacific to the USA and Canada, reminding the world that the Royal Navy was still the most impressive in the world.

Hood was ordered in response to the wartime German 28-knot Mackensen class battlecruisers, none of which were commissioned. Her design was modified in light of the lessons learned from the loss of battlecruisers *Queen Mary*, *Indefatigable* and *Invincible* at the Battle of Jutland, and extra armour was added. Although usually referred to as a battlecruiser, *Hood* was really a fast battleship and an improved version of the Queen Elizabeths, with the same main armament of eight 380mm/15in guns, a sloped armoured belt and improved torpedo protection. Nevertheless, magazine protection remained one of her weak spots and her deck armour was only 75mm/3in thick. Small-tube boilers and a longer hull-form gave *Hood* a speed of 31–2 knots, 7 knots faster than the Queen Elizabeths. However, the extra weight made her sit lower in the water than designed and she had a

ABOVE: *Hood* was made famous by her inter-war world cruise when she was admired for her handsome looks. She was sunk by the German battleship *Bismarck* after a few minutes' fight.

tendency to dig in, fore and aft, in any seaway and at speed. Four ships of the same class were originally ordered, but work on *Hood*'s three sisters, who were to be named *Rodney*, *Howe* and *Anson*, was halted in 1917.

Hood was modernized twice, once in 1929 and again in 1939. There were proposals to remove or reduce the 610-tonne/600-ton conning tower and make further improvements to her deck armour, but World War II came too soon to allow this.

Hood, marked with red, white and blue stripes to indicate her neutrality, was part of the international force which intervened in the Spanish Civil War. On St George's Day, 1937, *Hood* covered a convoy of three British merchant ships as they delivered food to the besieged population of Bilbao and evacuated refugees, training her guns on the Spanish Nationalist cruiser *Almirante Cervera* as she did so.

At the outbreak of World War II *Hood* was with the Home Fleet at Scapa Flow, taking part in the chase of *Scharnhorst* and *Gneisenau*, and escorting convoys in the North Atlantic. In June 1940 she was attached to Force H, the British force established at Gibraltar after the collapse of France and their commitment to defend the western Mediterranean. On July 3,

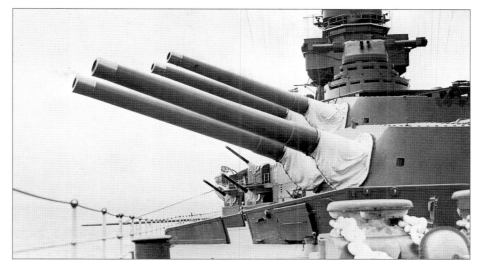

RIGHT: *Hood*'s main 380mm/15in guns and secondary armament trained out to starboard. BELOW: **Two sailors demonstrating loading drill on a 100mm/4in anti-aircraft gun.** BELOW RIGHT: **Nearly all battleships of the period had underwater torpedo tubes. Although much vaunted they were little used.** BOTTOM RIGHT: *Hood*'s crew of nearly 1,500 men required mass-catering on her mess deck.

1940, Force H opened fire on the French fleet at Mers-el-Kebir where the battleship *Bretagne* was blown up and *Provence* and *Dunkerque* were badly damaged.

In May 1941 *Hood* and the new *Prince of Wales* formed Vice Admiral Holland's Battle Cruiser Force sent to intercept the even newer German battleship *Bismarck* and the heavy cruiser *Prinz Eugen* as they made their breakout into the Atlantic. The Germans were found by the patrolling cruisers *Norfolk* and *Suffolk* and shadowed on radar. Reports by wireless enabled Holland to bring his ships into action on the morning of May 24 in the Denmark Strait, between Iceland and Greenland. Both sides opened fire shortly before 06.00 hours but as Holland closed the range *Bismarck*'s fifth salvo hit *Hood* amidships, starting a fire in her 100mm/4in ammunition. The fire spread to the main magazine, causing a catastrophic explosion which tore through the ship, breaking her hull in several places. Only three of her 1,418 ship's company survived.

The news shocked the British and the Prime Minister Winston Churchill ordered that "*Bismarck* must be sunk at all costs". The German ship had been damaged in the brief exchange of shot with *Hood* and *Prince of Wales*; two days later she was crippled by aircraft from the carrier *Ark Royal*, wrecked by the battleships *King George V* and *Rodney* on the morning of May 27, and finally despatched by torpedoes. Revenge was complete and commerce raiding by German surface warships was brought to an end.

Hood

Class: *Hood*. Launched 1918
Dimensions: Length – 262m/860ft
  Beam – 32m/105ft
  Draught – 8.7m/28ft 6in
Displacement: 43,355 tonnes/42,670 tons
Armament: Main – 8 x 380mm/15in guns
  Secondary – 12 x 140mm/5.5in, 4 x 100mm/4in
  guns and 6 x 535mm/21in torpedoes
Machinery: 24 boilers, 4 shafts.
  107,381kW/144,000shp
Speed: 31 knots
Complement: 1,477 men

Queen Elizabeth – modernized

The Queen Elizabeth class was reconstructed between the wars, emerging from the modernization with a single funnel, improved deck armour, additional anti-aircraft guns, and a hangar and catapult for two seaplanes.

In 1941 *Queen Elizabeth* joined the British Mediterranean Fleet at Alexandria where on December 19, 1941, she and *Valiant* were attacked by Italian frogmen. Both ships settled on an even keel and the extent of the damage was kept secret. *Queen Elizabeth* was repaired at Norfolk, Virginia, and *Valiant* at Durban in 1943, and later both ships bombarded Japanese positions in the Dutch East Indies. *Queen Elizabeth* was scrapped in Scotland in July 1945.

Valiant was modernized in 1929–30 and again in 1937–9, and in World War II served in every theatre of war: she took part in the Norway campaign in Spring 1940; she exchanged fire with the French battleship *Richelieu* at Dakar in September 1940 during an operation to put De Gaulle in power there; she fought at the Battles of Cape Matapan in March and Crete in May 1941; and provided covering fire during the Allied landings on Sicily in July and at Salerno in September 1943. In August 1944, *Valiant* was in dry dock at Trincomalee in Ceylon (now Sri Lanka) when the dock collapsed. She was never fully repaired and was sold for scrap in 1948.

At the Second Battle of Narvik in April 1940 *Warspite* led a flotilla of destroyers into the fjord where eight German destroyers and a U-boat were sunk. At the Battle of Calabria in July 1940, a single shot from *Warspite* hit the Italian battleship *Giulio Cesare* at nearly 24km/15 miles range and the Italian fleet retreated, however *Warspite* was too slow to catch up. At the Battle of Matapan in March 1941, *Warspite* sank two heavy cruisers. In the battle for Crete she was bombed and was sent to Puget Sound for repairs. In 1942 she was flagship of Force A in the Indian Ocean which brushed with Admiral Nagumo's Japanese fleet. She was hit by a German glider bomb during the Allied landings at Salerno in 1943, putting X turret out of action. Nevertheless, she bombarded the coast during the Normandy landings and again at Walcheren in 1944. *Warspite* was sold for scrap in early 1947, but broke her tow and ran aground in Mounts Bay, Cornwall, where she was eventually broken up.

On December 28, 1939, *Barham* was torpedoed by *U-30*, but repaired in Liverpool. She joined the Mediterranean Fleet and at the Battle of Matapan, she sank the Italian cruiser *Zara* and the destroyer *Alfieri* on the night of March 28, 1941. In May of that year, *Barham* was again severely damaged off Crete and repaired at Durban. Finally her luck ran out and on November 25, 1941, she was torpedoed by *U-331*. The German submarine was returning from having landed a small patrol to blow up a railway bridge on the Egyptian coast and her meeting with the *Barham* was by chance, her commanding officer doing well to get in a snap attack. *Barham* was hit by three torpedoes and within five minutes had rolled over to port,

LEFT: **An aerial view of one of the Queen Elizabeth class at anchor in Weymouth Bay: the number of small craft alongside and the work on deck hint at the logistic effort which each battleship needed, even in peacetime.** BELOW: **A multiple pom-pom or "Chicago piano" was retrofitted to many battleships for anti-aircraft defence. Note that the seamen wear knives on lanyards as their ancestors did in the age of sail.**

Queen Elizabeth class

Class: *Queen Elizabeth, Warspite, Valiant, Barham, Malaya.* Launched 1913–15

Dimensions: Length – 197m/645ft 9in
Beam – 27.6m/90ft 6in
Draught – 8.8m/28ft 9in

Displacement: 27,940 tonnes/27,500 tons

Armament: Main – 8 x 380mm/15in guns
in four twin turrets
Secondary – 16 x 150mm/6in, 2 x 75mm/3in
and 4 x 3pdr guns

Machinery: 24 boilers, 4 shafts.
55,928kW/75,000shp

Speed: 25 knots

Complement: 925 men

All ships of the class were extensively rebuilt
between the wars, and anti-aircraft
armament improved.

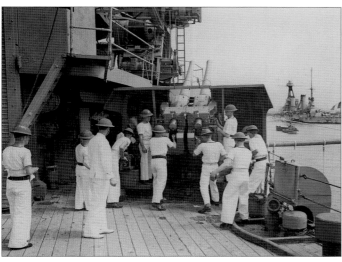

one or more of her magazines blew up and she sank with the loss of more than two-thirds of her crew. Cunningham acknowledged that the sinking of *Barham* was a most daring and brilliant performance on the part of the U-boat. He described the sinking:

I saw the Barham, *immediately astern of us, stopped and listing heavily over to port. The poor ship rolled nearly over on to her beam ends, and we saw men massing on her upturned side. A minute or two later there came the deep rumble of a terrific explosion as one of her main magazines blew up. The ship became completely hidden in a great cloud of yellowish-black smoke, which went on wreathing and eddying high into the sky. When it cleared away the* Barham *had disappeared. There was nothing but a bubbling, oily-looking patch on the calm surface of the sea, dotted with wreckage and the heads of swimmers. It was ghastly to look at, a horrible and awe-inspiring spectacle when one realized what it meant.*

TOP: **The end of *Barham*, torpedoed off Sollum on November 25, 1941.** ABOVE LEFT: **A gun crew at a drill while at anchor in Alexandria, 1940. The French battleship in the background would later be demilitarized.** ABOVE: **Even a 30,481-tonne/ 30,000-ton battleship could be moved by the waves. If the length matched the frequency of a wave, even a large ship could be moved like this.**

Malaya alone did not receive the second major refit like her sisters. She was at the Battle of Calabria, and then employed on escort duties in the North Atlantic. In March 1941, while escorting convoy SL67, *Malaya*'s aircraft spotted *Scharnhorst* and *Gneisenau* off the Cape Verde Islands, which turned away. Later she was torpedoed off the coast of West Africa by *U-106* and steamed to the USA for repairs. She ended her life moored in a Scottish loch as a stationary target for the RAF and was scrapped in 1948. *Malaya*'s ship's bell hangs in the East India Club, London.

Royal Sovereign class

Also known as the Revenge class, these ships were progressively modernized during their lives. *Revenge* and *Royal Oak* were the only ships of this class at the Battle of Jutland. They were envisaged as smaller versions of the Queen Elizabeths, designed to use coal or oil to fire the boilers. During and immediately after World War I the class received anti-torpedo bulges which increased their beam to 31m/102ft, director fire-control for the secondary armament, and flying-off ramps over B and X turrets. In the inter-war years various 150mm/6in guns were removed and replaced by 100mm/4in high-angle anti-aircraft guns. By 1939 the torpedo tubes and aircraft platforms were removed and anti-aircraft armament increased by two and later three octuple 2pdr mountings. Also the deck armour over the magazines was increased to 100mm/4in thickness. *Resistance*, *Renown* and *Repulse* were cancelled in 1914, but the steel which had been assembled for the latter two was used for two new battlecruisers of the same names. As a class they were too slow to be effective in World War II.

Ramillies and *Revenge* were deployed to Izmir during the brief Turko-Greek war after World War I. In 1939 *Ramillies* escorted troop convoys in the Channel and in 1940 in the Indian Ocean. On August 18, 1940, she bombarded Bardia, and in November fought at the Battle of Cape Spartivento while transferring from Alexandria to Gibraltar. She was escorting convoy HX106 when she was sighted by *Scharnhorst* and *Gneisenau* on February 8, 1941, and they turned away.

In May 1941 she took part in the hunt for *Bismarck*. By May 1942 she was back in the Indian Ocean where she bombarded Diego Suarez, but on May 20 she was torpedoed by a Japanese midget submarine. Repaired at Durban and at

TOP: ***Royal Sovereign* entering Malta in April 1935. Malta was the kingpin of British strategy in the central Mediterranean where the British had had interests since the 1600s.** ABOVE: **Three pictures on these two pages show the different camouflage schemes in use. These were intended not to disguise the ships but to fool the enemy's optical rangefinders. Here *Resolution* is in wartime camouflage in May 1942.**

Devonport, *Ramillies* bombarded German positions during D-Day and the Allied landings in southern France. She was sold for scrapping in 1948.

Revenge carried British bullion reserves to Canada in 1939 and escorted Canadian troopships back to England. In September 1940 *Revenge* bombarded Cherbourg to interrupt German preparations for Operation Sealion, the invasion of Britain. *Revenge* sailed from Halifax, Nova Scotia, to participate in the hunt for *Bismarck*. After a year in the Indian Ocean, *Revenge* returned home to be taken out of service and was sold for scrap in 1948.

Resolution also took bullion to Canada. During the Norway Campaign on May 18, 1940, she was hit by a large bomb which penetrated three decks, but was soon repaired. As part of Force H she bombarded the French fleet at Mers-el-Kebir on July 3, 1940. She took part in operations against the Vichy French at Dakar when she was torpedoed by the French submarine *Bévéziers*. When repairs at Portsmouth became impossible because of German air raids she was sent to Philadelphia. *Resolution* then escorted troop convoys in the

Royal Sovereign class

Class: *Ramillies, Resolution, Revenge* (ex-*Renown*),
Royal Oak, Royal Sovereign.
Launched 1914–16
Dimensions: Length – 190m/624ft
Beam – 27m/88ft 6in
Draught – 8.7m/28ft 6in
Displacement: 28,450 tonnes/28,000 tons
Armament: Main – 8 x 380mm/15in guns
Secondary – 14 x 150mm/6in guns and
4 x 535mm/21in torpedoes
Machinery: 18 boilers, 4 shafts.
29,828kW/40,000shp
Speed: 21 knots
Complement: 908–997 men

Indian Ocean, but by early 1944 had become a training ship
and was scrapped, also in 1948.

Royal Sovereign was in the Home Fleet during 1939 and on
Atlantic convoy duty in 1940–1. She was part of the British
Mediterranean Fleet at the Battle of Punto Stilo on July 18,
1940, when Cunningham, with the battleships *Warspite*,
Malaya, *Royal Sovereign*, and the carrier *Eagle*, met the two
Italian battleships *Giulio Cesare* and *Conte di Cavour*. *Warspite*
hit *Giulio Cesare* at long range, but Cunningham was hampered
by the slow speed of *Malaya* and *Royal Sovereign*, though he
pursued the Italians to within 80km/50 miles of the coast of
Calabria. *Royal Sovereign* spent 1942–3 refitting in the USA
after just one month in the Indian Ocean and then returned
home. On May 30, 1944, *Royal Sovereign* was loaned to the
Soviet navy and renamed *Arkhangelsk*. She was returned in
1949 and subsequently scrapped.

Royal Oak was sunk at Scapa Flow on October 14, 1939, by
the German submarine *U-47*, when 833 men were killed, the
wreck subsequently being preserved as a war grave. Recently,
divers have worked on the wreck to prevent leaking oil tanks
causing pollution.

One 380mm/15in gun from *Resolution* and another from
Ramillies are displayed outside the Imperial War Museum
in London.

Battle of Cape Spartivento

Operation Collar aimed to pass a fast convoy eastward through
the Mediterranean, which Admiral Somerville with Force H from
Gibraltar would cover with the battlecruiser *Renown* and the
carrier *Ark Royal*. Meanwhile aircraft carriers of the British
Mediterranean Fleet would raid targets as far apart as Tripoli

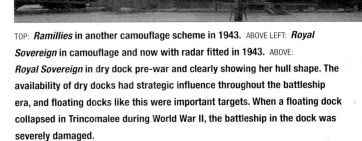

TOP: ***Ramillies** in another camouflage scheme in 1943.* ABOVE LEFT: ***Royal
Sovereign** in camouflage and now with radar fitted in 1943.* ABOVE:
***Royal Sovereign** in dry dock pre-war and clearly showing her hull shape. The
availability of dry docks had strategic influence throughout the battleship
era, and floating docks like this were important targets. When a floating dock
collapsed in Trincomalee during World War II, the battleship in the dock was
severely damaged.*

and Rhodes, and pass the battleship *Ramillies* through the
Mediterranean from east to west. Despite their setback at
Taranto earlier in November 1940, the Italian navy was still a
significant force, and when *Ramillies* was about to join Force H
off the coast of southern Sardinia, Somerville encountered a
superior Italian fleet including the battleships *Vittorio Veneto*
and *Giulio Cesare* and several cruisers.

The Battle of Cape Spartivento, or Tuelada as it is known
to the Italians, started with Somerville chasing towards the
Italians, but he was hampered by the slow speed of *Ramillies*,
and though shots were exchanged at long range, the British
could not overhaul the faster enemy. Air strikes also failed to
slow the Italians down. The battle ended when Somerville felt
obliged to turn back from the Italian coast to protect the
convoy. Curiously the British Admiralty ordered a board of
enquiry for not continuing the pursuit of the Italians, but
Somerville was exonerated.

LEFT: *Nelson* in the Thames for the Silver Jubilee in 1935. Ships of the fleet were anchored at various ports in the Thames to show themselves off to their public. The odd layout of these ships gave them a peculiar profile from wherever they were viewed.
ABOVE: *Nelson* and *Rodney* at sea together, bristling with guns.

Nelson and *Rodney*

The Royal Navy had various proposals for fast battleships or battlecruisers at the end of World War I, and *Nelson* and *Rodney* were lineal descendants of remarkable ships planned under the designation "G3". These plans were cancelled following the Washington Naval Treaty, but revived as heavy battleships incorporating the lessons learned in the war. However, the restriction on displacement to 35,560 tonnes/ 35,000 tons standard (a measure now defined for the first time by treaty) was in part responsible for their unusual layout of guns, which was intended to reduce the length of the armoured belt. The planned 119,312kW/160,000shp giving 30 knots was also reduced and they had only a quarter of that horsepower and the low speed of barely 23 knots.

The design aimed to produce the heaviest armament and best protection possible for the least displacement. They were amongst the best armoured of all British battleships with an internal belt of armour 305–355mm/12–14in thick, inclined at 15 degrees to the vertical and extending from A turret to the after 150mm/6in guns. The armoured deck was 165mm/6.5in over the magazines and 95mm/3.75in thick over the machinery, not including the 25mm/1in plating underneath.

The internal bulges were designed to withstand a 340kg/ 750lb warhead, and comprised an empty outer chamber, a water-filled chamber, a 38mm/1.5in torpedo bulkhead inboard and another compartment to limit flooding if the torpedo

bulkhead was strained. *Nelson*'s armour was further increased in 1937–8. Triple drum boilers enabled the actual number of boilers to be reduced to eight.

The three triple turrets were all forward of the superstructure, with B turret at a higher level than A and C. The 150mm/6in guns on either beam repeated this arrangement. In World War II a large number of smaller-calibre guns were added, especially the octuple 2pdr known as a "Chicago piano" and single 20mm/0.79in guns. Initially the 405mm/16in guns suffered some mechanical problems which compared badly to the tried and tested British 380mm/15in gun, and the power-operated 150mm/6in and 120mm/4.7in guns were slow. The performance of all these guns had improved by the outbreak of World War II.

Some other navies copied features of *Nelson* and *Rodney*. On rebuild the USN's *Idaho*, *Mississippi* and *New Mexico* were given tower masts, the French *Dunkerque* and *Strasbourg* were given Nelson-like gun layouts, and the Japanese and Russian navies also toyed with similar designs.

In October 1939 when Germany tried to repeat a World War I tactic by sailing the battlecruiser *Gneisenau* and other ships to draw the Home Fleet within U-boat range, *Nelson* and *Rodney* with *Hood*, *Repulse*, *Royal Oak* and the carrier *Furious* searched but made no contact with the enemy. When the armed merchant cruiser *Rawalpindi* was sunk on November 23

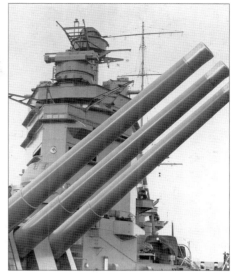

ABOVE LEFT: **The triple 405mm/16in guns of *Nelson* and her ship's company preparing for inspection.** ABOVE RIGHT: ***Nelson*'s main armament at maximum elevation.** LEFT: ***Rodney*, an Admiral class battleship of 1884, showing how far battleship design had come in 50 years.** BELOW: ***Rodney* ammunitioning with 405mm/16in shells, a slow, cumbersome, manpower-intensive task and the techniques were little improved since the days of sail.**

by *Scharnhorst* and *Gneisenau*, *Nelson* was one of the ships which prevented their breakout into the Atlantic, but returning to base she was damaged by a mine laid by *U-31* off Loch Ewe. Once repaired, *Nelson* joined Force H and was part of the escort for most of the important Malta-bound convoys in 1941 and 1942, although on September 27, 1941, during Operation Halberd, she was damaged by an Italian aircraft torpedo. *Nelson* was repaired well in time for Operation Torch, the Allied landing in North Africa in November 1942 and in July 1943. Together with *Rodney*, *Warspite* and *Valiant*, she was part of a fleet of over 2,500 American and British warships assembled for the invasion of Sicily.

One of the bombarding ships during the Normandy landings, *Nelson* was damaged by a mine on June 18, 1944. Repaired in Philadelphia, she briefly saw action in the Far East before becoming a training ship. She was used as a target ship in 1948 and scrapped in 1949.

Rodney had a similar wartime career to *Nelson*, except she took part in the Norway Campaign in 1940, where she was hit by a large bomb which penetrated three decks but did not explode. Her most famous action was the sinking of *Bismarck*. On May 27, 1941, *King George V* and *Rodney* caught up with the crippled German battleship and opening fire at about 08.45 reduced *Bismarck* to a wreck in an hour and a half, thus avenging the loss of *Hood*.

Nelson and *Rodney*

Class: *Nelson, Rodney.* Launched 1925
Dimensions: Length – 216m/710ft
   Beam – 32m/106ft
   Draught – 10m/33ft 6in
Displacement: 33,848 tonnes/33,313 tons
Armament: Main – 9 x 405mm/16in guns
   Secondary – 12 x 150mm/6in, 6 x 120mm/4.7in
   guns and 2 x 620mm/24.5in torpedoes
Machinery: 8 boilers, 2 shafts.
   33,557kW/45,000shp
Speed: 23 knots
Complement: 1,314 men
Rodney was larger at 33,370 tons and both ships at deep load were well over 40,000 tons

King George V class

The King George V class were designed just as the inter-war naval treaties expired, and the Royal Navy needed modern fast ships to match the German *Bismarck* and *Tirpitz*. The critical path for construction lay through the manufacture of guns, which the British had been trying to limit to 355mm/14in as they thought this the optimum size to fit into a treaty-sized 35,560-tonne/35,000-ton hull. The arrangement of two quadruple turrets, fore and aft, and a double turret in B position was a trade-off between armament and armour.

The secondary armament consisted of a new 130mm/5.25in dual-purpose gun mounted in eight twin power-operated turrets, and the other, lighter close-range anti-aircraft weaponry was upgraded during the war by fitting eight-barrelled pom-poms and 20mm/0.79in guns. Some ships were fitted with a rocket, which fired a trailing wire and an explosive

charge, but this proved more dangerous to the firer than to any enemy aircraft. Armoured protection was better than in the Nelsons, including the anti-torpedo bulges being divided into a sandwich, the middle layer being used for fuel or water. They had four shafts each driven by an independent set of machinery, and space-saving Admiralty pattern three-drum boilers. Speed to catch the enemy was important, and the class was designed to reach 27.5 knots, 6 knots faster than *Nelson* and *Rodney*.

As a class they were commissioned in the war, decommissioned in the late 1940s and scrapped in 1957–8, a life of about 16 years. *King George V* was completed in October 1940 and in March 1941 covered a commando raid on the Lofoten islands. She then covered convoys in the North Atlantic and Arctic and, on May 27, 1941, while flagship of the British Home Fleet, she brought *Bismarck* to bay. Churchill had ordered that *Bismarck* must be sunk at all costs and suggested that this might mean towing *King George V* home, but the order was as unnecessary as it was unusual. She gave gunfire support during the landings on Sicily and at Salerno in 1943,

BELOW: **King George VI visiting the battleship named after his father "in northern waters" during World War II. A comparison (see opposite) with a similar view of an earlier ship of the same name shows how far warship construction and equipment had advanced in 20 years.**

King George V class

Class: *King George V, Prince of Wales, Duke of York, Anson, Howe.* Launched 1939–40
Dimensions: Length – 227m/745ft
Beam – 31m/103ft
Draught – 8.9m/29ft
Displacement: 37,316 tonnes/36,727 tons
Armament: Main – 10 x 355mm/14in guns
Secondary – 16 x 130mm/5.25in and
32 x 2pdr guns
Machinery: 8 boilers, 4 shafts.
82,027kW/110,000shp
Speed: 28 knots
Complement: 1,422 men

ABOVE FAR LEFT: **An aerial view of one of the class underway.**
ABOVE LEFT: **King George VI is seen here inspecting his father's namesake.** LEFT: **By comparison the World War I battleship called *King George V* (scrapped in the 1920s) had torpedo nets, very little fire control equipment when first built, and a stern gallery which was a design feature left over from the days of sail. Radar, of course, was not available until World War II.**

and in December brought Churchill home from the Tehran Conference. *King George V* was refitted before joining the British Pacific Fleet in October 1944, and was in Tokyo Bay at the Japanese surrender on September 2, 1945.

Duke of York was ready for service in November 1941, was employed on Arctic convoys, and covered the landings in North Africa in October 1942. In December 1943 she was covering convoy JW55B when the German battlecruiser *Scharnhorst* sortied from her lair in the Norwegian fjords. On December 26, in appalling weather, *Duke of York*'s radar-controlled guns scored several hits on *Scharnhorst,* enabling the escorting cruisers to torpedo the German battlecruiser. *Duke of York* was flagship of the British Pacific Fleet at the Japanese surrender.

Howe covered Arctic convoys until May 1943, but in July she transferred to the Mediterranean for the invasion of Sicily. In 1944 she became flagship of the British Pacific Fleet during the Okinawa campaign, in the new role for the battleship of bombardment and providing an anti-aircraft umbrella for the fleet. In June 1945 she was sent into dock at Durban and so missed the Japanese surrender. *Anson* covered Arctic convoys until June 1944, when she was sent to Plymouth for refit. In

April 1945 *Anson* and the *Duke of York* sailed for the Far East and on August 30, 1945, *Anson* helped liberate Hong Kong two days before the formal Japanese surrender at Tokyo. *Anson* never fired her 355mm/14in guns in anger.

When *Bismarck* escaped from the Norwegian fjords into the Atlantic she was intercepted, on May 24, 1941, in the Denmark Strait by *Hood* and *Prince of Wales*. *Hood* blew up after a brief engagement. *Bismarck* shifted her fire on to *Prince of Wales* and damaged her, but not before *Prince of Wales* had hit *Bismarck,* causing damage and fuel leaks which led eventually to the German ship's demise.

In August 1941, *Prince of Wales* took Churchill across the Atlantic to meet President Roosevelt in Newfoundland, where together they drafted the first Atlantic Charter. Later that year *Prince of Wales* together with *Repulse* formed Force Z at Singapore, which sailed to stop Japanese troops landing on the Malay coast. On December 10, 1941, Force Z was overwhelmed by Japanese bombers and torpedo aircraft: they were the last two American or British capital ships in the Pacific. Following Pearl Harbor, air power, which the British Fleet Air Arm had done so much to develop in the Mediterranean, had truly come of age.

Lion class and *Vanguard*

This four-ship class of battleships was an enlarged version of the King George V class and was contemplated pre-war with two ships, *Lion* and *Temeraire*, being laid down in 1939. Under the London Naval Treaty these ships would have had 405mm/16in guns on a 45,720-tonne/45,000-ton displacement. Similar in layout and silhouette the Lion class would have had a transom stern, an armoured conning tower and a pole mainmast. The turbines and boilers were arranged as in *King George V*, but the 405mm/16in gun would have been a development over *Nelson*'s guns, with a shell 15 per cent heavier. Construction was suspended on the outbreak of World War II and cancelled in 1943–4. The Royal Navy realized very early that the era of the battleship was drawing to a close.

Vanguard was the last battleship to be built for the Royal Navy. Built on Clydebank, she was launched on November 30, 1944, but did not serve in the war. She was the biggest British battleship with a deep load displacement of 51,820 tonnes/51,000 tons. Her guns were reputedly those of *Glorious* and *Courageous* and had been in storage since the 1920s when it was decided to convert the ships to aircraft carriers.

The heavy anti-aircraft armament was what might be expected for war in the Pacific, but soon after the end of World War II many of the single 40mm/1.57in guns were removed. In 1947, when *Vanguard* took part in a royal tour to South Africa by King George VI, the anti-aircraft mounting above B turret was replaced by a reviewing platform.

Vanguard was refitted at Devonport in 1947–8, and then used as a training ship at Portsmouth where she became something of a fixture. She was sold for scrapping in 1960, and thousands of people gathered to wave farewell to this icon of British sea power on August 6. As *Vanguard* was being towed out through the narrow entrance to Portsmouth harbour, she broke free of her tugs and threatened to crash into a public house on the Portsmouth side and cut through the Custom House jetty. However she ran aground. She was towed off later that day, and finally scrapped at Faslane just a few miles from Clydebank where she was built. This was the end of an era. For reasons of cost, manpower, technical advance and operations, the world's greatest navy gave up the construction of battleships forever.

ABOVE: *Vanguard*, the last battleship of a long line in the Royal Navy – although outwardly different, she was similar to the King George V class. TOP LEFT: A handsome picture of *Vanguard* from the air. TOP RIGHT: *Vanguard* from the stern, a view which the architect seems to have neglected, but the transom stern was intended to increase her length and, with a pronounced sheer to the bow, to give her better seagoing qualities. RIGHT: *Vanguard* dressed overall and beautifully framed.

Vanguard

Class: *Vanguard*. Launched 1944

Dimensions: Length – 248m/814ft 4in
    Beam – 33m/108ft
    Draught – 9.4m/30ft 9in

Displacement: 45,215 tonnes/44,500 tons

Armament: Main – 8 x 380mm/15in guns
    Secondary – 16 x 130mm/5.25in and
    73 x 40mm/1.57in guns

Machinery: 8 boilers, 4 shafts.
    96,941kW/130,000shp

Speed: 30 knots

Complement: 1,893 men

Colorado class

Four ships were ordered in 1916 and were completed in the 1920s, apart from *Washington*, which was never finished, and represented the first 405mm/16in battleships of the USN. Apart from the size of the guns, the design and layout of the Colorado class were an evolution of the Tennessee class, and like all USN battleships were characterized by lattice masts. *Maryland* was the first American battleship to be fitted with a catapult. Later these ships carried three catapults, two on the quarterdeck and one on X turret.

Modernization for all three ships was approved in 1939, but rising tension worldwide delayed this until 1941. Modernization had started at Puget Sound on *Colorado*, when *Maryland* and *West Virginia* were sunk at Pearl Harbor, but both were raised and also went to Puget Sound for their delayed modernizations. They emerged in 1942 with additional armour and anti-torpedo bulges. Further refits during the war progressively improved the radars, gunnery directors and anti-aircraft armament.

Colorado returned after her refit to Pearl Harbor in August 1942. From December 1942 to September 1943 she was deployed in the New Hebrides and the Fiji islands as part of a blocking force against further Japanese expansion. In November 1943 she provided gunfire support for the American landings on Tarawa, and was then sent back to the USA for a further upgrade. During early 1944 *Colorado* covered landing operations at Kwajalein, Eniwetok, Saipan, Guam and Tinian. At Tinian on July 24, shore batteries found her range and she

ABOVE: ***Colorado*** **passes under the Golden Gate bridge into San Francisco in 1945. This iconic scene was repeated many times over – and continues to be so – but for many ships at the end of World War II it was also a last scene as the USN was run down and ships placed in reserve during the post-war period.**

was hit 22 times. Repaired on the West Coast, *Colorado* arrived in Leyte Gulf where on November 27 she was hit by two kamikazes. Many of the ship's crew were killed or wounded and the attack caused extensive damage. Nevertheless, a few days later she bombarded Mindoro in December before going to Manus Island for temporary repairs. Off Luzon in January 1945, *Colorado* bombarded Japanese positions in Lingayen Gulf where she was hit once more. In April and May 1945 *Colorado* covered the invasion of Okinawa and in August and September was in Tokyo Bay. At the end of the war, in a repeat of the use of USN battleships after World War I, *Colorado* made "magic carpet" voyages, bringing over 6,000 troops home. She was placed in reserve in 1947 and sold for scrapping in 1959.

At Pearl Harbor *Maryland* was berthed inboard of *Oklahoma* and thus was protected from the fury of the attack. Although hit by bombs she was able to steam to Puget Sound after temporary repairs. The pattern of employment for all this class of ships was dictated by their age and lack of speed, and since they were too slow to operate with the aircraft carriers, *Maryland*, though repaired at Puget Sound in two months, missed the main actions of the Battle of Midway. Later

TOP LEFT: **A Colorado class battleship, with storeships alongside, is preparing for her next action. This picture is reminiscent of many others: battleships with their huge crews were hungry beasts with a constant demand for stores.** ABOVE: ***Maryland* firing point-blank during the bombardment of Tarawa.** LEFT: ***Colorado* firing her 405mm/16in guns to starboard, sometime in the 1940s. Note how the technique of lattice mast construction has been retained.** BELOW: **Skills like signalling with flags survived even the age of the battleship. One sailor is sending semaphore and another is reading a message: in ideal conditions this method could be used at the extremes of visibility.**

Maryland joined *Colorado* in protecting the routes to Australia through the Fiji islands and the New Hebrides. Her main role during the extensive amphibious campaigning in the Pacific was to provide gunfire support, as she did at Tarawa in the Gilberts, at Kwajalein Atoll in the Marshalls and at Saipan.

On June 22, 1944, while at anchor off Saipan, a Japanese aircraft missed *Pennsylvania* but torpedoed *Maryland*, opening a gaping hole in her side. Nevertheless she was repaired at Pearl Harbor within two months and was ready to cover beach clearance operations in the Palau islands.

On October 25,1944, *Maryland* took part in the Battle of Surigao, part of the larger Battle of Leyte Gulf, when the Japanese battleships *Fuso* and *Yamashiro* tried to force the straits. The Japanese were detected by a layered defence of torpedo boats, destroyers, cruisers and battleships, and the remnants of the Japanese force were then annihilated by naval aircraft.

In November *Maryland* was hit by a kamikaze plane which crashed between A and B turrets. Again repaired at Pearl Harbor, *Maryland* was back for the Okinawa campaign, where on April 7, a kamikaze plane hit her, this time on X turret causing heavy casualties, especially amongst the exposed 20mm/0.79in gunners. *Maryland* was sent back to Puget Sound for permanent repairs and was there on VJ-Day. On the "magic carpet" run she brought back more than 8,000 troops. Placed in reserve in 1947, *Maryland* was scrapped in 1959.

Colorado class (continued)

ABOVE: **A dramatic picture of _Maryland_ in the thick of action in November 1944. The action was not at night, but the brightness of the explosion on _Maryland's_ forecastle has resulted in the film being under-exposed. Nevertheless, the melodramatic mood of the picture is accurate.**

At Pearl Harbor on December 7, 1941, _West Virginia_ lay in battleship row, berthed outboard of _Tennessee_, where in the first waves of attack she was hit by seven 455mm/18in aircraft torpedoes in her port side and two bombs. The bombs caused fires and the detonation of ammunition, wrecking two of _West Virginia's_ aircraft and setting light to their aviation fuel. The torpedoes badly damaged the port side but prompt damage control prevented her capsizing. _West Virginia's_ captain was killed by shrapnel from a bomb landing on _Tennessee_. _West Virginia_ settled on an even keel and fires drove her crew off the ship: others were trapped below decks and suffered a lingering death. The fires were only subdued after 24 hours and she was refloated six months later to be rebuilt at Puget Sound over the next two years.

Like her sisters, the lattice masts were removed, a new superstructure was fitted and a very large number of 40mm/ 1.57in and 20mm/0.79in anti-aircraft guns fitted. The 125mm/ 5in guns in casemates were also replaced by dual-purpose 125mm/5in guns in turrets. The two funnels were trunked into one, giving _West Virginia_ a very different silhouette to other ships of the class.

At the Battle of Surigao _West Virginia_ led _Maryland_, _Mississippi_, _Tennessee_, _California_ and _Pennsylvania_ in a line that, for the last time in history, crossed the T of the enemy's line, and sank the Japanese battleship _Fuso_. Other operations included covering the landings in Lingayen Bay and the invasions of Iwo Jima and Okinawa, finishing in Tokyo Bay on August 31, 1945. After this _West Virginia_ played host to thousands of visitors for Navy Day on October 27 in San Diego,

and was part of the "magic carpet" bringing home thousands of US servicemen. The "Wee Vee" was decommissioned in the late 1940s and sold for scrapping in 1959.

The Battle of Leyte Gulf

This action arose from a Japanese attempt to interrupt American troop-landings there. A Northern Decoy Force with four carriers (but not many aircraft) and two partially converted battleship-carriers steamed south from Japan. A Centre Strike Force including five battleships closed Leyte Gulf from the north-west through San Bernadino Strait, while a Southern Strike Force including two battleships closed from the south-west through the Surigao Straits in a pincer.

On October 24, in the Battle of Sibuyan Sea, the Centre Strike Force was attacked by aircraft of the US Third Fleet, and the giant battleship _Musashi_ was sunk. Next the Northern Decoy Force succeeded in luring the Third Fleet north leaving the San Bernadino Strait open, with only escort carriers and old battleships of the US Seventh Fleet to protect the landings.

Overnight on October 24/25, the Southern Strike Force of the battleships _Fuso_ and _Yamashiro_ entered the Surigao Strait where they suffered successive attacks from smaller ships, during which _Yamashiro_ was lost. When _Fuso_ met six US battleships formed into line she too was sunk.

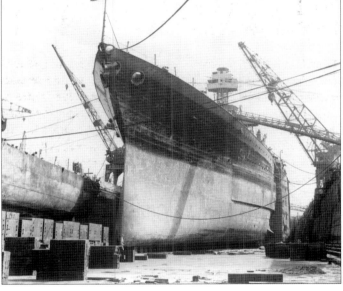

LEFT: *West Virginia* on fire and aground after being torpedoed in battleship row, Pearl Harbor, 1941. BELOW: After the Japanese attack, *West Virginia* was raised and repaired and she is seen here in dry dock, June 1942. The recovery and repair of ships after the Japanese attack on Pearl Harbor became a matter of pride for the USN, even after it was realized that aircraft carriers were needed more than battleships.

ABOVE: **The incomplete battleship *Washington* in 1922. She was destined to be sunk in experiments during 1924. The name was used in a new ship of a subsequent class.**

Early on October 25, the remains of the Centre Strike Force with four battleships steamed through the San Bernardino Strait to attack the escort carriers and accompanying destroyers of the Seventh Fleet. Japanese surface ships and kamikaze aircraft sank or destroyed two escort carriers and several smaller ships, but just when the Centre Strike Force should have smashed the amphibious shipping, the Japanese turned away.

Meanwhile at the Battle of Cape Enga, aircraft of the US Third Fleet sank all the main units of the Northern Decoy Force, *Chitose*, *Chiyoda*, *Zuiho* and *Zuikaku*. Centre Strike Force, having failed in its objective, escaped from the returning US Third Fleet.

Colorado class

Class: *Maryland, Colorado, Washington, West Virginia.* Launched 1920–1
Dimensions: Length – 190m/624ft
Beam – 29.7m/97ft 5in
Draught – 9.2m/30ft 2in
Displacement: 33,123 tonnes/32,600 tons
Armament: Main – 8 x 405mm/16in guns
Secondary – 12 x 125mm/5in, 8 x 75mm/3in guns and 2 x 535mm/21in torpedoes
Machinery: 8 boilers, 4 shafts.
19,985kW/26,800shp
Speed: 21 knots
Complement: 1,083 men

North Carolina class

The name North Carolina was taken from a ship ordered in 1917, laid down in 1920, but cancelled under the terms of the Washington Naval Treaty.

In the new *North Carolina* the armament was increased from 355mm/14in to 405mm/16in during their design, but too late to alter other features of the class. However, for the first time in a USN ship the guns were arranged two forward and one aft, with secondary armament in turrets. There were no scuttles in the hull and habitability suffered accordingly. Their hulls had to be strengthened after both ships experienced severe vibrations on trials and during World War II both were refitted, when they received enclosed bridges, improved radars, and a very large number of anti-aircraft guns. Post-war there were proposals to convert *North Carolina* and *Washington* into satellite launch ships, helicopter ships, or fast-replenishment ships but these came to nothing.

North Carolina was the first of her class to be built after the expiry of the Washington Naval Treaty in 1936. She was regarded as the first of the modern battleships, receiving so much publicity that she was nicknamed "Showboat".

When the Pearl Harbor attack took place *North Carolina* was undergoing trials off the East Coast of America. She entered the Pacific in June 1942 and covered the landings at Guadalcanal and Tulagi in August 1942. The USN had developed the concept of battle groups consisting of carriers and battleships, in which long-range strike capability was provided by the carrier's aircraft and the purpose of the battleship was as an anti-aircraft battery. In this role, *North Carolina* was on the screen of the aircraft carrier *Enterprise* during the Battle of the Solomons, August 23–25. During this

ABOVE: *North Carolina* photographed in 1941. The USN battleships of this class were the first to be built after the expiry of the Washington Treaty. This picture shows *North Carolina* as she was designed and built, but very soon afterwards she was taken in hand again and fitted with a massive anti-aircraft armament, radars and improved fire-control systems.

engagement *North Carolina* claimed to have shot down between seven and fourteen Japanese aircraft in one eight-minute action. On September 6, 1942, *North Carolina* was torpedoed by a Japanese submarine but she was repaired at Pearl Harbor and ready for action in November.

From then on *North Carolina*'s actions read like a roll call of the American island-hopping advance through the Pacific: Tarawa, Makin, Kwajalein, Majuro, Truk, Marianas, Palau, Yap, Ulithi, Woleai, Ponape, Satawan, New Guinea, Wake, Saipan and the Battle of the Philippine Sea.

In 1945 during preparations for the landings on Okinawa, *North Carolina* played the battleship's dual role of providing heavy bombardment and an anti-aircraft umbrella. On April 6 while under attack by kamikaze aircraft she was hit by friendly fire and needed repairs at Pearl Harbor before joining a carrier battle group for the attack on the Japanese home islands. In the final days of the assault she bombarded factories near Tokyo, and she landed seamen and marines ashore for "preliminary occupation duty".

North Carolina provided the "magic carpet" for troops on passage between Okinawa and the US East Coast, made one training cruise for midshipmen and was then deactivated. In 1961 she was given to the people of North Carolina, where she is now a museum ship at Wilmington.

LEFT: *North Carolina*'s launch in June 1940. ABOVE: *Washington*, equipped with all her wartime additions. BELOW LEFT: *North Carolina* on her maiden voyage, but apparently not yet fully fitted, showing off the elevation of her guns.

North Carolina class

Class: *North Carolina, Washington.* Launched 1940
Dimensions: Length – 222m/728ft 9in
 Beam – 33m/108ft 4in
 Draught – 10m/33ft
Displacement: 38,086 tonnes/37,484 tons
Armament: Main – 9 x 405mm/16in guns
 Secondary – 20 x 125mm/5in, 16 x 28mm/1.1in
 and 12 x 13mm/0.5in guns
Machinery: 8 boilers, 4 shafts.
 90,230kW/121,000shp
Speed: 28 knots
Complement: 1,880 men

A battleship named *Washington* was ordered in 1916 but cancelled in 1921 when the hull was already built, and she was sunk as a target in 1924. In the early part of 1942 the new battleship *Washington* was deployed in the North Atlantic and Arctic with the British Home Fleet. On May 1, *King George V* rammed the British destroyer *Punjabi,* cutting her in two, and *Washington* passed between the sinking halves while *Punjabi*'s depth charges exploded beneath her. *Washington* escaped with only a minor leak and whip damage to her fire-control radars.

In August 1942 *Washington* entered the Pacific, and on the night of November 14–15 took part in a battle off Savo Island. The Japanese were trying to reprovision their positions at Guadalcanal when *Washington* and *South Dakota* met the Japanese battleship *Kirishima* in a night action. *Kirishima* concentrated her fire on *South Dakota* who was forced to retire, but was badly damaged by *Washington*'s accurate radar-controlled gunnery and had to be scuttled the next

morning. This was the only battleship-to-battleship action that took place during World War II.

Washington was involved in another collision in February 1943 when she rammed *Indiana*, crumpling her bows. A temporary bow was fitted at Pearl Harbor and she was sent to Puget Sound for permanent repair. From then on *Washington* formed part of various carrier battle groups and took part in the Battle of the Philippine Sea in June 1944 when together with six other battleships, four heavy cruisers, and 14 destroyers she formed the screen.

Like other battleships, *Washington*'s anti-aircraft armament was steadily improved throughout the war until by the end she sported 15 x quadruple 40mm/1.57in, 1 x quadruple 20mm/0.79in, 8 x twin 20mm/0.79in, and 63 x single 20mm/0.79in guns. *Washington*'s last refit carried her through VJ-Day and she made only one brief sortie into the Pacific before being sent to Europe to bring troops home. She was decommissioned in 1947, and scrapped in 1961.

South Dakota class

This class generally resembled the North Carolinas but were shorter and more heavily armoured as they were designed to provide protection against 405mm/16in shells, but on the same displacement as the earlier ships, and with the same speed and armament. Two ships were planned and two more added to the programme at the outbreak of World War II in Europe. Underwater, the outboard propeller shafts were encased in fins and the inboard shafts were placed entirely between the fins. Overall the design was rather cramped, causing problems of habitability between decks and operationally for the placing of anti-aircraft guns around the superstructure. All four ships were ready for service in 1942.

During the war the 28mm/1.1in and 13mm/0.5in anti-aircraft guns were replaced with larger numbers of 40mm/1.57in and 20mm/0.79in weapons. In addition, the radar suite was upgraded and the bridges were enclosed. Like other battleships post-war plans were made for conversion to missile ships, satellite launch ships, helicopter assault ships, and fast replenishment ships, but none of these ideas came to fruition.

South Dakota was fitted as a force flagship and her conning tower was one level higher than other ships of the class, compensating for the extra weight by having two fewer 125mm/5in guns and an extra pair of quadruple 28mm/1.1in guns. She made an inauspicious start on September 6, 1942, when she struck an uncharted pinnacle in Lahai Passage and suffered extensive damage to her hull needing several weeks of repairs at Pearl Harbor.

In October 1942 South Dakota was part of a battle group centred on the carriers Enterprise and Hornet which met a much larger Japanese carrier force preparing for a major assault on Henderson Field. In what became known as the

TOP: **South Dakota taken on August 9, 1943. In this picture South Dakota's anti-aircraft armament has been greatly increased over her original design.** ABOVE: **South Dakota in line astern somewhere in the Pacific in 1945. There was no other formation in which the number of guns bearing on a target could be maximized.**

Battle of Santa Cruz, Hornet was sunk and Enterprise was temporarily put out of action while the Japanese carrier Shokaku was damaged. While protecting Enterprise during the third wave of air attacks, South Dakota was hit on her A turret by a 227kg/500lb bomb, but she was also credited with having shot down 26 Japanese planes.

On October 30, South Dakota and the destroyer Mahan were in collision and South Dakota's bows crumpled, requiring a repair at Noumea. However, by November 13, 1942, she was able to join the battleship Washington and four destroyers for a night sweep off Guadalcanal, while a Japanese flotilla consisting of the battleship Kirishima, several cruisers and destroyers were approaching to bombard Henderson Field.

In the moonlight of November 14/15, the enemy were sighted from South Dakota at a range of 16,550m/18,100yds. Washington opened fire shortly before South Dakota and the salvoes from both ships straddled the Japanese. South Dakota then fired on another target until it disappeared from her radar screen. As South Dakota's after main turret fired on a third target, it demolished her own planes, whilst her 125mm/5in

TOP LEFT: **Colours on the last evening as *South Dakota* is decommissioned (the guns under the dome are already "mothballed").** ABOVE: ***South Dakota* manoeuvring while under air attack from a Japanese Kamikaze aircraft.** FAR LEFT: **The guns of *Indiana* on commissioning day, April 30, 1942.** LEFT: **One of the South Dakota class firing her broadside at a shore target. Despite all the investment in battleships, this and anti-aircraft defence was, at the end of their era, their principal role.**

guns engaged targets close inshore, thought to be enemy destroyers. *South Dakota* was then illuminated by searchlight at about 5,485m/6,000yds from ships as they cleared Savo Island, and she came under fire from several warships including the battleship *Kirishima*, taking considerable damage. A fire started in the foremast, she lost power temporarily, her radios failed, her radars and radar plot were demolished, and, as she turned away from the onslaught, she lost track of her consort. *Washington* continued the engagement, damaging *Kirishima* so badly that the Japanese scuttled her next morning. The Americans lost three destroyers, the Japanese cruisers *Takao* and *Atago* were hit and, besides *Kirishima*, the destroyer *Ayanami* was also scuttled.

South Dakota was again repaired at Noumea and she was sent to New York for refit in December 1942. For a few months she operated in the North Atlantic as convoy escort before returning to the Pacific in September 1943, where the actions she was involved in were the familiar roll-call of the American advance across the Pacific. On June 19, 1944, the first day of the Battle of the Philippine Sea, the battleship escorts were

placed so as to be able to continue supporting the army and marines on Saipan while being prepared to intercept a Japanese surface force which was known to be approaching from the west. *South Dakota* was hit during a heavy air raid by a 227kg/500lb bomb which penetrated the main deck, causing minor material damage but over 50 casualties. However, her damage control was sufficient to keep her in action until she was sent to Puget Sound for repair in July.

In May 1945, while loading ammunition from a stores ship, an explosion caused a fire and her magazines were flooded to prevent further damage. Then on July 14, *South Dakota* bombarded the Kamaishi Steel Works on Honshu, the first time that the home islands of Japan had been attacked by ships since the Royal Navy had bombarded Shimonseki and Kagoshima in the 19th century.

South Dakota was in Tokyo Bay for the formal Japanese surrender, leaving there on September 20, 1945, to be refitted in Philadelphia in 1946. In 1962, after 15 years in reserve, she was sold for scrapping. A wave of nostalgia meant that other ships of her vintage were preserved as museum ships.

South Dakota class (continued)

Indiana operated in the Pacific throughout World War II. From November 1942 to October 1943 she was part of a fast battle group based around the carriers *Enterprise* and *Saratoga* as the Americans advanced through the Solomons. In November 1943 she was part of the force which re-took the Gilbert Islands, and in January 1944 she bombarded Kwajalein for eight days prior to the landings there. However, on February 1 *Indiana* collided with the battleship *Washington* and needed repairs to her starboard side at Pearl Harbor.

In the Battle of the Philippine Sea, she bombarded Saipan on June 13–14 and on June 19 as four large air raids attacked the American ships, *Indiana* helped the other escorts and the carrier-based fighters shoot down 100 of the enemy in what was called the "Great Marianas Turkey Shoot". In the next months she bombarded targets on Palau and the Philippines, was refitted at Puget Sound, resumed her bombardment role at Iwo Jima and Ulithi, and screened the carriers during raids on Tokyo in February 1945. Between March and June 1945 she supported carrier operations against Japan and Okinawa,

BELOW: **The USN took part in amphibious operations in Europe as well as the Pacific. Here the *Massachusetts* prepares for Operation Torch off the coast of North Africa.**

riding out a terrible typhoon in June. In August she bombarded targets on the Japanese home islands, and on September 5 entered Tokyo Bay. Later she formed part of the Pacific Reserve Fleet until being sold for scrap in 1962. *Indiana*'s mast is erected at the University of Indiana in Bloomington and her anchor is on display at Fort Wayne.

Massachusetts was commissioned in May 1942 and supported the Allied landings in North Africa, Operation Torch, in November 1942. On November 8, off Casablanca, she silenced the guns of French battleship *Jean Bart* and sank two French destroyers. *Massachusetts* was then deployed to the Pacific, first covering the route through the Solomons to Australia, and then in November 1943 escorting the carrier strikes on the Gilbert Islands. In December she shelled Japanese positions on Nauru and in January she bombarded Kwajalein. Other operations followed at Truk, Saipan, Tinian, Guam and again at Truk, and she was at the Battle of Leyte Gulf in October 1944.

Massachusetts experienced the tremendous typhoon in December 1944, with winds estimated at 120 knots, in which three destroyers foundered. In June 1945 she passed through the eye of a typhoon with 100-knot winds. In July and August 1945 she shelled targets on the Japanese mainland, probably

firing in anger the last 405mm/16in shell of World War II on August 9. Since 1965, "Big Mamie", as she is known, has been a museum ship at Fall River, Massachusetts.

Alabama formed part of the British Home Fleet, based in Scapa Flow from May to August 1943, while British battleships were employed in the Mediterranean in support of the Allied landings on Sicily. In June, Alabama and her sister ship covered the reinforcement of Spitzbergen. In July, Alabama feinted at southern Norway aiming to reinforce German beliefs of a threatened landing there, and perhaps to lure the German battleship Tirpitz from her lair in the fjords.

By late 1943 Alabama was in the thick of the fighting in the Pacific, including the Battles of the Philippine Sea and Leyte Gulf, and the bombardment of Japan itself. On August 15, 1945, when the Japanese capitulated, Alabama's seamen and marines were among the first American forces to land.

Her war was over when she had retrieved her crew on September 5, in Tokyo Bay, and taken 700 members of the USN's construction battalion home from Okinawa, arriving in San Francisco on October 15, 1945. In 1962 Alabama became a museum ship at Mobile, Alabama.

TOP LEFT: **The brand-new *Alabama* in camouflage in December 1942.**
TOP RIGHT: **A stoker puts on a burner of one of *Alabama*'s boilers.** ABOVE FAR LEFT: **A close-up of one of *Alabama*'s 405mm/16in guns.** ABOVE LEFT: **Another view of the business end of *Alabama*.** ABOVE RIGHT: **Old and new technology. Two fire control radars, a direction-finding loop, and signal flags. Flag signals, under the right circumstances, were still a reliable and adequate means of sending orders.**

South Dakota class

Class: *South Dakota, Indiana, Massachusetts, Alabama.* Launched 1941–2
Dimensions: Length – 207m/680ft
Beam – 33m/108ft
Draught – 10.7m/35ft
Displacement: 38,580 tonnes/37,970 tons
Armament: Main – 9 x 405mm/16in guns
Secondary – 20 x 125mm/5in and
numerous lighter guns
Machinery: 8 boilers, 4 shafts.
96,941kW/130,000shp
Speed: 27.5 knots
Complement: 1,793 men

LEFT: **Post-war much of the tertiary armament of anti-aircraft guns was removed to produce the clean lines of *Iowa*.** BELOW: **The business of ammunitioning ships did not however end. After a series of disastrous explosions earlier in the century caused by unstable ammunition, it was now normally inert, but was still stowed quickly.**

Iowa class and *Iowa*

The Iowas were the last class of battleships to be completed for the USN and were considered to be the best, certainly the fastest, and with their long forecastles, cowled funnels and relatively low silhouettes, among the most handsome of all their type. They were conceived as stretched versions of the South Dakotas, their length (60m/200ft longer) giving them 5 to 6 knots extra speed (despite an increase of 10,160 tonnes/ 10,000 tons standard displacement) and making them capable of protecting a force of fast carriers against the swift Japanese Kongo class battlecruisers.

The USN invoked the so-called escalator clause of the London Naval Treaty to exceed the 45,720-tonne/45,000-ton limit, and eventually the full load displacement of these ships was 58,460 tonnes/57,540 tons. Four ships were planned and two more added in January 1941 after the Japanese attack on Pearl Harbor in the previous month.

Although designed to counter Japanese heavy cruisers and battlecruisers, their principal roles were as command ships, in-shore bombardment, and, of course, operating in fast carrier battle groups as air defence ships for which they were fitted with a huge number of anti-aircraft guns (the actual numbers varied from ship to ship). They underwent the same World War II modifications as other American battleships, including improved electronics, an enlarged and enclosed bridge and yet more anti-aircraft guns.

They were prestigious vessels capable of a number of tasks, but like nearly every other Dreadnought their war complement was much greater than their peacetime complement. *Iowa*, for example, carried 1,000 more men than her given number of 1,921. They were thus expensive ships to maintain in service and though recalled to service in Korea, Vietnam and the Gulf War for their bombardment capability, they were frequently placed in reserve.

When *New Jersey* was recalled for the Vietnam War, where the air threat was minimal, even though all of the 40mm/1.57in and 20mm/0.79in guns were removed, she still needed a complement of over 1,500 to man the main armament and the steam plant. Even when fitted with eight quadruple armoured boxed launchers for Tomahawk cruise missiles and four quadruple canisters for Harpoon surface-to-surface missiles, their very high manpower costs could not be justified. However, in testimony to the powerful iconic status of these

Iowa class

🇺🇸

Class: *Iowa, New Jersey, Missouri, Wisconsin, Illinois, Kentucky.*
Launched 1942–50

Dimensions: Length – 270m/887ft
Beam – 33m/108ft
Draught – 11m/36ft 2in

Displacement: 48,880 tonnes/48,110 tons

Armament: Main – 9 x 405mm/16in guns
Secondary – 20 x 125mm/5in, 80 x
40mm/1.57in and 50 x 20mm/0.79in guns

Machinery: 8 boilers, 4 shafts.
158,088kW/212,000shp

Speed: 33 knots

Complement: 1,921 men

ABOVE: *Iowa* firing her main armament. LEFT: The fire and smoke of a broadside. There was noise too. RIGHT: The blast effect can clearly be seen on the surface of the sea. There was always a risk of self-inflicted damage from blast. These two aerial photographs show, by the flattening of the water around *Iowa*, how far the blast effect reached.

ships, even in the late 1990s some of them were notionally held in reserve, though there was very little probability of them returning to service.

Besides Tomahawk and Harpoon missiles and modern close-in weapons systems, other options included designating them as BBGs or guided-missile battleships but it was realized that the missiles were unlikely to withstand the blast effects of the 405mm/16in guns. They were not modernized for the Korean War, but in the 1980s the electronics were upgraded, the catapults and aircraft were replaced with limited helicopter facilities, and drone launch and recovery systems were fitted. The aircraft crane was suppressed and habitability was improved. They were not, however, refitted as flagships.

As a class they were finally decommissioned in 1990–2. *New Jersey* and *Wisconsin* both still had reserve status in 1996, but *New Jersey* was stricken in 1999 to allow her to become a museum at Camden, New Jersey, and *Wisconsin* is a "museum-in-reserve" at Norfolk, Virginia. *Missouri* is a museum at Pearl Harbor, and *Iowa*, who has been robbed for spares for the other ships, lies at Suisun Bay, California, awaiting preservation.

Iowa was specially fitted as a flagship and her conning tower was one deck higher than her sisters, who nevertheless proved equally capable of the role. She was damaged by grounding on her trials and repaired at Boston. She took President Franklin D. Roosevelt to Casablanca in 1943 on his way to the Tehran Conference, and when she had brought him back she transferred to the Pacific where she operated in support of fast-carrier task forces for the remainder of the war. *Iowa* also bombarded the Japanese home islands in July 1945 and she entered Tokyo Bay with the occupation forces on August 29, 1945.

Iowa was placed in reserve in 1949, re-commissioned in 1951–8, and made one deployment in the Korean War when she bombarded North Korean positions. She was modernized and commissioned again in 1984, but in 1989 her B turret was damaged by an internal explosion, and the centre gun was never restored. Despite being used for spares, she was reinstated on the register of naval vessels in 1999, but after years lying at Philadelphia she was towed to California to be a museum. Besides the *Mikasa* in Japan, and some shipwrecks, all the preserved battleships of the modern era are in the USA.

New Jersey

The second *New Jersey*, and the first of three similar ships built in the same yard, was launched at the Philadelphia Naval Shipyard on the anniversary of the Japanese attack on Pearl Harbor. She transited the Panama Canal in January 1944 to join the US Fifth Fleet which was in the Ellis Islands, preparing for the assault on the Marshall Islands. Her first employment was screening a carrier task force as they flew strikes against Kwajalein and Eniwetok. On January 31, the Fifth Fleet landed troops on two atolls, the undefended Majuro and the bitterly defended Kwajalein. The stubborn Japanese defence continued well into the month, while US forces assaulted another atoll, Eniwetok, on January 17. When the Japanese threatened to mount relief operations by forces based at Truk 1,127km/700 miles away, *New Jersey*, now flagship of the Fifth Fleet, led a raid which successfully disrupted their operations.

In June *New Jersey* supported the American invasion of the Marianas. The Japanese fleet was ordered to annihilate the American invasion force, which led to the Battle of the Philippine Sea, also known as the "Marianas Turkey Shoot" because the Japanese lost so many of their aircraft. *New Jersey*'s role was in providing anti-aircraft close support to the

ABOVE: **USN battleships survived post-war and ships such as *New Jersey*, seen here with a modern suite of electronics, was used to bombard shore targets during the Vietnam War. Here *New Jersey*, photographed in March 1960, is seen firing on targets near Tuyho in central South Vietnam.**

carriers. The loss of some 400 aircraft, three carriers and many trained pilots was a disaster for the Japanese. Following this *New Jersey* became flagship of the Third Fleet as fast carrier task forces struck at targets throughout the theatre of war. In September the targets were in the Visayas and the southern Philippines, then Manila and Cavite, Panay, Negros, Leyte and Cebu. Raids on Okinawa and Formosa (now Taiwan) to debilitate enemy air power began in October in preparation for landings at Leyte.

This invasion brought about the last major sortie of the Imperial Japanese Navy in a three-pronged attack. In the Battle of Leyte, a Northern Decoy Force of carriers, though nearly bereft of aircraft, and two battleships succeeded in drawing away ships which should have been protecting the invasion beaches. This allowed the Japanese Centre and Southern Strike Forces to close Leyte Gulf through the San Bernardino Strait. Both were heavily damaged, but the Centre Strike Force,

RIGHT: **New Jersey in the Pacific in November 1944. Compare the suite of aerials with those on the opposite page.** BELOW: **Long Beach Naval Shipyard, California. Overhead view of the aft deck of the battleship New Jersey in dry dock while undergoing refitting and reactivation.** BELOW RIGHT: **The perspective of this photograph emphasizes the long bow of this class of ships even more.**

New Jersey

Class: *Iowa, New Jersey, Missouri, Wisconsin, Illinois, Kentucky.* Launched 1942–50
Dimensions: Length – 270m/887ft
    Beam – 33m/108ft
    Draught – 11m/36ft 2in
Displacement: 48,880 tonnes/48,110 tons
Armament: Main – 9 x 405mm/16in guns
    Secondary – 20 x 125mm/5in, 80 x
    40mm/1.57in and 50 x 20mm/0.79in guns
Machinery: 8 boilers, 4 shafts.
    158,088kW/212,000shp
Speed: 33 knots
Complement: 1,921 men

despite losing the giant battleship *Musashi*, entered the area of amphibious operations. Meanwhile *New Jersey* had gone north and although the Third Fleet sank the decoy force, the landings were at risk. *New Jersey* returned south at full speed, but the Centre Strike Force too had turned back and made its escape. Japan now intensified its suicide attacks and on October 27, in the mêlée which characterized mass kamikaze attacks, *New Jersey* damaged a plane, which crashed into the carrier *Intrepid* while anti-aircraft fire from *Intrepid* sprayed *New Jersey*.

In December 1944 *New Jersey* was part of the Lexington task force which attacked Luzon and then experienced the same typhoon which sank three destroyers.

New Jersey continued her roles at Iwo Jima and Okinawa and off Honshu before a refit at Puget Sound, and from September 17, 1945, to January 28, 1946, she was guardship in Tokyo Bay. Notably, by the end of the war, her anti-aircraft armament consisted of 20 x quadruple 40mm/1.57in, 8 x twin 20mm/0.79in, and 41 x single 20mm/0.79in guns.

Between periods in reserve *New Jersey* saw much post-war action. She twice deployed to Korea, in the familiar role of giving gunfire support ashore, though on several occasions the

Koreans reached her with their own shore batteries, and she also operated with Allied warships, notably the British cruiser *Belfast* and the Australian carrier *Sydney* in October 1951.

In the 1960s she was refitted for the Vietnam War, and in operations off the coast of Vietnam *New Jersey* fired some 3,000 405mm/16in shells.

New Jersey was also uniquely engaged in support of US marines in Beirut in February 1984 when she fired nearly 300 rounds into the surrounding hills. Proponents of the battleship argued that they still had a viable role and that with armour more than 305mm/12in thick in many places even an Exocet-type missile would bounce off.

In 1986 *New Jersey*'s deployment in the Pacific was used to support the case for the battleship battle group concept and the battleship modernization programme was validated. Consequently in 1987–8 *New Jersey* visited Korea prior to the Olympic Games, and Australia during the bicentennial there, and exercised in the Indian Ocean and the Gulf. She was decommissioned for the last time in 1991 at Bremerton, which had seen so many battleships during World War II. *New Jersey* opened as a museum ship and memorial in October 2001.

Missouri

*M*issouri, or the "Mighty Mo", was not ready until the very end of 1944. Her first operations were to escort the carriers of Task Force 58 on strikes on the Japanese islands, and to bombard Iwo Jima. In March 1945 she opened the Okinawa campaign by bombarding the island. During the Battle of the East China Sea, on April 7, Missouri was escorting the carriers of the US Fifth Fleet which sank the giant Japanese battleship *Yamato*, a cruiser and four destroyers.

In June and again in July *Missouri* and other ships bombarded Japanese industrial targets on the home islands, and by the end of July the Japanese no longer had control over their own sea and air space. On August 10, the Japanese sued for peace and while negotiations were underway the Commander-in-Chief of the British Pacific Fleet, Admiral Fraser, conferred an honorary knighthood on Admiral Halsey on August 16. On August 21, *Missouri* landed 200 men for duty with the initial occupation force and she entered Tokyo Bay on August 29, where the surrender took place onboard on September 2, 1945.

In the months immediately after the war, *Missouri* attended celebrations in New York, carried the remains of the Turkish ambassador to the USA to Istanbul, and balanced this with a

ABOVE RIGHT: *Missouri* in action. The area of disturbed water indicates the extent of the blast from the guns. There were similar blast effects on the upper deck of the ship. BELOW: *Missouri* experienced war in the Pacific and was heavily engaged post-World War II as well. She is now preserved as a museum ship.

visit to Greece. This Mediterranean deployment, lasting until the spring of 1946, was the beginning of a long-term USN commitment to defend the region against Soviet expansion and marked an early stage in the Cold War.

Following this, on September 2, 1947, President Truman celebrated the signing of the Inter-American Conference for the Maintenance of Hemisphere Peace and Security. This extension of the 19th-century Monroe doctrine marked the decline of British naval influence in the region. Truman and his family returned to the USA in *Missouri*.

On January 17, 1950, *Missouri* spectacularly ran aground in Hampton Roads, her momentum carrying her three ship-lengths out of the main channel and lifting her some 2m/7ft above the waterline. She was re-floated two weeks later.

The Korean War was business as usual for *Missouri*. In September 1950 she bombarded shore targets and from

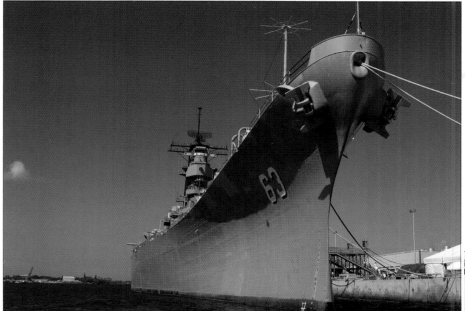

Missouri

Class: *Iowa, New Jersey, Missouri, Wisconsin, Illinois, Kentucky.* Launched 1942–50

Dimensions: Length – 270m/887ft
Beam – 33m/108ft
Draught – 11m/36ft 2in

Displacement: 48,880 tonnes/48,110 tons

Armament: Main – 9 x 405mm/16in guns
Secondary – 20 x 125mm/5in, 80 x
40mm/1.57in and 50 x 20mm/0.79in guns

Machinery: 8 boilers, 4 shafts.
158,088kW/212,000shp

Speed: 33 knots

Complement: 1,921 men

TOP: **The fine long bows which were features of this generation of USN battleships.** ABOVE: **USN sailors and marines witness the Japanese surrender ceremony onboard the battleship *Missouri* in Tokyo Bay.** RIGHT: **The orderly scene around the table of the signing ceremony contrasted sharply with how it must have looked to the Japanese, with USN sailors and marines hanging from every vantage point in the ship.**

then until March 1951 her duties alternated between more bombardments and air defence of carrier task forces. On December 23, 1950, she gave gunfire support to the Hungnam defence perimeter as the last US troops were evacuated.

After two midshipmen's training cruises and a refit which lasted until January 1952, *Missouri* returned to Korea, where her last bombardment was against targets in the Kojo area on March 25, 1953. She was placed in reserve in February 1955, where she remained for nearly 30 years. In 1984–6 she was refitted to help make up the 600-ship USN and in the autumn of 1986 sent on a circumnavigation, following the track of the Great White Fleet. When she emerged from refit her 20 125mm/5in guns had been reduced to 12 and replaced with 32 Tomahawk cruise missiles and 16 Harpoon surface-to-surface missiles. All the 40mm/1.57in and 20mm/0.79in anti-aircraft

guns had been suppressed. In the late 1980s *Missouri* was based in the Pacific, deployed to the Gulf area during an incipient crisis there, and took part in numerous exercises.

After Iraq invaded Kuwait on August 2, 1990, *Missouri* was sent via Hawaii and the Philippines to the Gulf. On January 17, 1991, *Missouri*'s mission was yet again shore bombardment, but this time the weapons used were 28 Tomahawk cruise missiles. In February *Missouri* also used her 405mm/16in guns, the first time they had been fired in anger for nearly 40 years.

At Pearl Harbor on December 7, 1991, *Missouri* took part in a commemoration of the 50th anniversary of the attack there, and she was decommissioned for the last time on March 31, 1992. In 1998 the "Mighty Mo" was given to the USS *Missouri* Memorial Association and opened as a museum ship on January 29, 1999.

LEFT: **A standard aerial three-quarters bow-on shot of *Wisconsin* in the Hampton Roads, showing the battleship in its ultimate state of development. Heavy guns are in place, but a considerable secondary and tertiary armament has been added to give the ship better defence against smaller surface ships and, of course, aircraft.** ABOVE: **Three of the USN's four remaining Dreadnoughts in reserve at Philadelphia Navy Yard during 1967: from left to right, *Wisconsin*, *New Jersey* and *Iowa*. The end of an era, even for the USN, is at hand.**

Wisconsin

The new *Wisconsin* joined the Pacific War in October 1944, screening the fast carriers during operations against the Philippines, Formosa, Lingayen Gulf and French Indo-China. After bombarding Manila on December 18th *Wisconsin* and the fleet were caught by a typhoon when the ships were short of fuel and light in the water; three destroyers were sunk. Her next operation was the occupation of Luzon and anti-aircraft escort for the air strikes on Formosa, Luzon and the islands of Nansei Shoto in January 1945. She also made a sweep of the South China Sea, in the hope that Japanese heavy ships might be met at sea. In February, when Task Force 58 attacked the Japanese home island, under the cover of bad weather *Wisconsin* escorted the main body of ships, and she was at Iwo Jima also in February and Okinawa in March 1945.

When the 66,040-tonne/65,000-ton battleship *Yamato* attacked the American invasion fleet off Okinawa on April 7, she was sunk by carrier planes and *Wisconsin* was not called into action. Meanwhile the US fleet came increasingly under attack from kamikaze aircraft making suicide dives, and on April 12 it was estimated that about 150 enemy aircraft were destroyed in the "divine wind" as *Wisconsin* kept most of the kamikazes away from their targets. In June *Wisconsin* rode out a typhoon, while two carriers, three cruisers and a destroyer

suffered serious weather damage. Operations against Japan resumed on June 8, when the Japanese air effort was already broken. Consequently on July 15 *Wisconsin* was able to close with the coast and bombard steel mills and refineries on Hokkaido, and industrial plant on Honshu, even closer to Tokyo. Battleships of the British Pacific Fleet joined the bombardment.

When *Wisconsin* anchored in Tokyo Bay on September 5, she had already steamed over 160,900km/100,000 miles during her short career. In the immediate post-war period *Wisconsin* provided the "magic carpet" for returning US servicemen, paid visits to South America and cruised with midshipmen embarked to Europe until 1947.

Wisconsin spent two years in reserve until required for the Korean War, where she replaced her sister ship *New Jersey* as flagship of the Seventh Fleet. Operations included screening the carrier attack forces, and as the air threat diminished, frequently joining the "bombline" to provide gunfire support to forces ashore. Targets included artillery positions, bunkers, command posts, harbours, railways, shipyards and trench systems, and on one occasion the illumination with star-shell of an enemy attack. On March 15, 1952, one of *Wisconsin*'s last missions in the Korean War was to destroy a troop train, but she in turn was hit by four 150mm/6in rounds from a shore

Wisconsin

Class: *Iowa, New Jersey, Missouri, Wisconsin, Illinois, Kentucky.* Launched 1942–50
Dimensions: Length – 270m/887ft
    Beam – 33m/108ft
    Draught – 11m/36ft 2in
Displacement: 48,880 tonnes/48,110 tons
Armament: Main – 9 x 405mm/16in guns
    Secondary – 20 x 125mm/5in, 80 x
    40mm/1.57in and 50 x 20mm/0.79in guns
Machinery: 8 boilers, 4 shafts.
    158,088kW/212,000shp
Speed: 33 knots
Complement: 1,921 men

TOP: **Wisconsin refuelling a destroyer underway in February 1945.** ABOVE: **An informal band concert onboard.** RIGHT: **The beginning of the end of one of the class, whose guns have been cut off but not yet hoisted away for recycling.**

battery. Three seamen were injured but little material damage was done. On April 4 and 5 at Guam, as a test, *Wisconsin* became the first Iowa class battleship to enter a floating dock.

Wisconsin remained in commission throughout the 1950s, alternately employed in training and on exercises, and showing the flag in the Atlantic and Pacific. On May 6, 1956, *Wisconsin* collided with the destroyer *Eaton* in a heavy fog. The long, relatively thin bows of these ships were graceful, but a weakness of the design meant that the collision badly damaged *Wisconsin*. In order to hasten repairs the 109-tonne/120-ton, 20.7m/68ft-long bow of the uncompleted *Kentucky* was brought by barge from Newport News to Norfolk, welded in place in a remarkable 16 days, and on June 28 she was ready.

What was thought to be *Wisconsin*'s last deployment in 1956–7 consisted of a midshipmen's training cruise and exercises, visiting Western Europe, the West Indies and the Mediterranean. When *Wisconsin* joined the reserve fleet in 1958, it was the first time since 1895 that the USN had had no battleship in commission. With *Iowa*, she remained at Philadelphia for 26 years until refitted to help make up the Reagan era's 600-ship navy. The 125mm/5in guns were replaced by surface-to-surface missiles and the 40mm/1.57in and 20mm/0.79in guns by 20mm/0.79in radar-controlled,

automatic Phalanx guns. On a typical training cruise she would embark up to 700 midshipmen from colleges across the USA, and visit ports in northern Europe or the Mediterranean and the West Indies. On her penultimate cruise *Wisconsin* sailed from Norfolk on June 19, 1957, transited the Panama Canal, crossed the Equator and visited Chile, whilst on her last cruise she visited the Clyde in Scotland in September and Brest in France. The USN decommissioned *Wisconsin* in 1990, but she was almost immediately required for the 1990–1 Gulf War. With *Missouri*, *Wisconsin* bombarded targets north of Khafji in Saudi Arabia, on Faylaka Island and in Kuwait City.

She was decommissioned for the final time on September 30, 1991, and after languishing in the navy yard *Wisconsin* was berthed in 2000 in downtown Norfolk as a museum ship.

Kentucky and *Illinois*

LEFT: *Kentucky* and *Illinois* were never completed. The bow of *Kentucky* was used to repair *Wisconsin*, and although redesigned several times while building, the hull never progressed much beyond the stage seen here.

Two other ships of the Iowa class were ordered. Originally *Kentucky* and *Illinois* were to have been of the new Montana type but the USN opted for an existing design, the Iowa.

Kentucky was laid down in March 1942 but, when in June the priority for construction became large numbers of landing craft, the double bottom section of the ship was launched and towed away. Work resumed in December 1944 but proceeded slowly and in 1947, when nearly half-finished, work stopped again, restarted briefly in 1948 and stopped again. The hull was re-launched in 1950 to clear the dock for repairs to *Missouri* after her grounding.

Kentucky was redesigned several times in the late 1940s and 1950s, and was designated as BBG-1, a missile-firing ship. However, her bow was cut off in May 1956 to repair *Wisconsin* after her collision. A replacement bow was built but never fitted. She was scrapped in 1959 when her engines and boilers were salvaged and installed in two fast combat-support ships.

The order for *Illinois* was cancelled in 1945, at the end of World War II.

Alaska class

LEFT: Although designated in the USN as CB, indicating a cruiser, these ships carried 305mm/12in guns and were battleships in all but name. They were not, however, regarded as a successful type.

Although armed with 305mm/12-in guns, the Alaska class was more like the heavy cruisers, or "pocket battleships" built without treaty limits, than regular, heavily armoured battleships. They were built to counter the threat of Japanese commerce raiders, a threat that never materialized.

Alaska entered the Pacific theatre in December 1944, when her primary task was to provide an anti-aircraft fire screen for the fast-carrier task forces formed around the fleet carriers *Yorktown*, *Intrepid*, *Independence* and *Langley*. *Alaska*'s secondary role was to direct fighters. *Alaska* destroyed her first

kamikaze on March 18, 1945, but also shot down a friendly aircraft. Next day she escorted the heavily damaged carrier *Franklin* out of the fray. On March 27, in her third role, she also bombarded targets on Okinawa. After a busy summer she made a sweep into the East China Sea in July to find that it was empty of enemy ships, and then in August operated against the Japanese mainland.

However, in September, October and November 1945 *Alaska* supported the landing of occupying troops at Inchon in Korea and Tsingtao in China, who took over from Japanese garrisons.

Alaska was expensive in manpower, and by the end of the war there were plenty of cruisers which could perform her roles. She went into reserve in 1946–7 and was never reactivated, being sold for scrap in 1960.

Guam, who operated mainly with *Alaska* in the Pacific, was likewise placed in reserve in 1947 and sold for scrapping in 1961. It was proposed to convert *Hawaii* to a guided-missile ship and then to a command ship, but she was never finished.

Alaska class

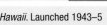

Class: *Alaska, Guam, Hawaii*. Launched 1943–5
Dimensions: Length – 246.5m/808ft 6in
  Beam – 27.8m/91ft 1in
  Draught – 9.7m/31ft 10in
Displacement: 30,257 tonnes/29,779 tons
Armament: Main – 9 x 305mm/12in guns
  Secondary – 12 x 125mm/5in, 56 x
  40mm/1.57in and 34 x 20mm/0.79in guns
Machinery: 8 boilers, 4 shafts.
  111,855kW/150,000shp
Speed: 33 knots
Complement: 1,517 men

Montana class

The USN planned five ships of the Montana class: they would have been 282m/925ft long and 37m/121ft in the beam and, freed of treaty limits, the size grew quickly from 45,700 tonnes/ 45,000 tons to over 60,950 tonnes/ 60,000 tons displacement. With 8 boilers generating 128,260kW/172,000shp their designed speed was 28 knots. Originally 455mm/18in guns were considered but the USN settled for 12 405mm/16in guns in four triple turrets. A new large-calibre 125mm/5in gun was planned and they would have had a plethora of 40mm/ 1.57in and 20mm/0.79in guns.

Heavily armoured and bulged, they would not have fitted through the Panama Canal at the time and money was included in the budget to build new locks along the waterway.

Construction work was halted in April 1942, on the grounds of steel shortages, and *Montana*, *Ohio*, *Maine*, *New Hampshire* and *Louisiana* were cancelled on July 21, 1943. The Battle of Midway had shown, as had in different ways the war at sea in the Atlantic and the Mediterranean, that the future need was for aircraft carriers. Consequently the planned Montana class of battleships was cancelled and their place in the USN's construction plans was taken by six carriers of the Midway class.

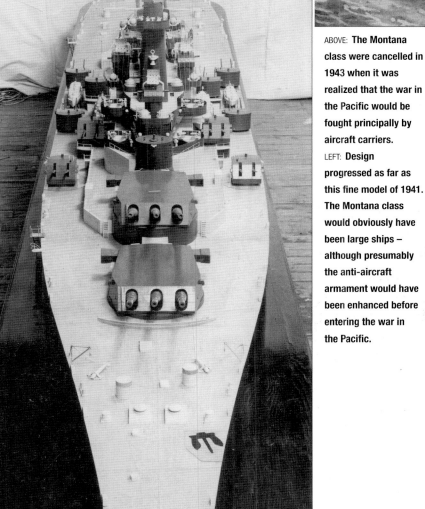

ABOVE: **The Montana class were cancelled in 1943 when it was realized that the war in the Pacific would be fought principally by aircraft carriers.**

LEFT: **Design progressed as far as this fine model of 1941. The Montana class would obviously have been large ships – although presumably the anti-aircraft armament would have been enhanced before entering the war in the Pacific.**

Nagato and *Mutsu*

Built between 1917 and 1920 the Nagato class were the first all-Japanese-designed warships, the first to be fitted with 405mm/16in guns, and at the time among the fastest battleships in the world. At this stage of international relations the Japanese still had access to British technology and were able to learn the lessons of Jutland: *Nagato* and *Mutsu* were regarded as equivalent to the British Queen Elizabeth class.

Both were modified in 1924 and rebuilt in 1934–5. A characteristic of *Nagato*'s appearance was the six-legged mast festooned with platforms. However, smoke from the fore funnel interfered with the gunnery control positions and in 1921 a tall cowl was added. Later, at the first conversion, the fore funnel was given a distinctive S-shape. Various positions were tried for aircraft ramps and catapults, which aid the dating of photographs.

In 1934 the horizontal armour was reinforced, anti-torpedo bulges were fitted and extended beyond the armoured citadel, the torpedo tubes were removed and there were various additional platforms built around the foremast. New engines and boilers were fitted which allowed there to be one massive central funnel, and the length was increased by extending the stern 8.7m/28.5ft. The heavy guns were given greater elevation (and thus range) and numerous lighter guns were added. Finally an aircraft catapult and crane were added at the weather deck or X turret deck level.

ABOVE: **Designed during World War I but completed in the 1920s, *Nagato* is seen here during her early trials. The massive conning tower is clearly Japanese, but Japanese naval architects had been trained in Britain, and there are still traces of that influence in *Nagato*'s profile, particularly her upright funnels.**

In 1941 *Nagato* was Yamamoto's flagship during the attack on Pearl Harbor. She also took part in the Battles of Midway, the Philippine Sea, and Leyte Gulf.

In May and June 1942 Yamamoto with some 150 ships set out to occupy Midway Island and the western Aleutians, hoping to draw out the US Pacific Fleet to its destruction. As Dutch Harbor in the Aleutians was being invaded by the Japanese, the main carrier battle raged in the south between groups of aircraft carriers. Four Japanese carriers were lost: *Akagi*, *Hiryu*, *Kaga* and *Soryu*, on June 4 and 5, and the American *Yorktown* was badly damaged and sunk by a Japanese submarine on June 7. Yamamoto had spread his forces too widely, and although outnumbered the Americans had been able to concentrate their forces better. The Battle of Midway was the first major victory for the USN in the Pacific. Afterwards the Japanese still had the most ships, including aircraft carriers, but the industrial muscle of the USA would soon change this. So, when *Nagato* and the Japanese fleet retreated from Midway, it marked the high tide of attempts to secure the perimeter of their conquests.

Nagato class

Class: *Nagato, Mutsu.* Launched 1919–20
Dimensions: Length – 216m/708ft
 Beam – 29m/95ft
 Draught – 9m/30ft
Displacement: 34,340 tonnes/33,800 tons
Armament: Main – 8 x 405mm/16in guns
 Secondary – 20 x 140mm/5.5in, 4 x 80mm/3.1in
 guns and 8 x 535mm/21in torpedoes
Machinery: 15 oil-burning and 6 mixed-firing
 boilers, 4 shafts. 59,656kW/80,000shp
Speed: 26.5 knots
Complement: 1,333 men

Two years later the Battle of the Philippine Sea was also fought at long range and although it involved *Nagato*, as well as four other Japanese battleships, these retreated after disastrous losses of Japanese aircraft.

However, during the Battle of Leyte Gulf, on October 25, 1944, *Nagato* was one of four battleships of the Japanese main Centre Strike Force which passed through the San Bernadino Strait into the amphibious area of operations. There at the Battle of Samar, *Nagato* sank the escort carrier *Gambier Bay* and three destroyers. Kamikaze aircraft also sank the escort carrier *St Lo*, but instead of wreaking havoc among the amphibious shipping, the Centre Strike Force retired through the San Bernadino Strait.

Nagato having been damaged by aircraft bombs off Samar was temporarily repaired, but did not see action again. She was bombed at Yokosuka on July 18, 1945, and badly damaged, and when the Japanese surrendered she was the last surviving battleship afloat. Her end was ignominious: while under tow to Bikini atoll she and her escort broke down and drifted for two days. She had developed a leak and was listing

TOP: *Nagato* or *Mutsu* after her refit of 1924 and before the 1933–4 refit.
ABOVE LEFT: The Japanese fleet leaving Brunei on October 22, 1944, en route to their defeat at the Battle of Leyte: from right to left, *Nagato, Musashi, Yamato* and cruisers. ABOVE RIGHT: The Japanese *Nagato* seen in the late 1930s preparing for aircraft operations by hoisting a biplane on to a launching ramp on B turret. However, once the war started such aircraft were mostly dispensed with and battleships relied on their carrier escorts for aerial reconnaisance.

and needed three weeks' repairs before she could complete her voyage. However, she survived the first (atmospheric) nuclear test, codename Able, with fairly minor damage, but sank from massive hull damage after the second (underwater), test, codename Baker, on July 25, 1946.

Mutsu was paid for by popular subscription, much of it raised in schools. She survived the cuts imposed on the Japanese Navy by the Washington Treaty, and took part in the attack on Pearl Harbor, the Battle of Midway and the Solomons campaign. However, on June 8, 1943, whilst in Hiroshima Bay, an explosion in the after magazine blew *Mutsu* in two. The cause has never been satisfactorily explained.

Kaga and *Tosa*

After the Russo-Japanese War the Imperial Japanese Navy, with much of its fleet obsolescent notwithstanding its victory at Tsushima, developed the concept of the 8-8 fleet. The Japanese had already thought of the all-big-gun ship when they received news from Portsmouth of Fisher's *Dreadnought* and their 8-8 concept laid emphasis on large, fast battleships. Their idea was that there were ages of ships, the first in the front line, the second operational but aging, and the third in reserve. The concept was that they would have two squadrons of eight ships, each less than eight years old, backed by ships of the other ages. This plan, with variations due to changes of government, finance and international tension, was maintained until the Washington Naval Conference. Meanwhile the Japanese concept had become the 8-8-8 plan, one squadron of ships of each age, and this called for four more battleships and four battlecruisers by 1928. Japan was spending more than one-third of her national budget on naval construction, and it is unlikely that she could have achieved the 8-8-8 plan, but she was resentful at the limits imposed by the Washington Naval Treaty in 1921–2.

The treaty called for the cancellation of *Kaga* and *Tosa*, both laid down in 1920. They were conceived as high-speed battleships with the same speed as the Nagatos but with the main armament increased to ten 405mm/16in guns with an X

ABOVE: **There are no pictures of *Kaga* or *Tosa* as fast battleships, but there are images of hybrid aircraft carriers like *Ise*, seen here in 1943.**

and a Y turret. When cancelled in 1922 under the Washington Naval Treaty, *Tosa* was used for explosives trials and sunk as a target ship in 1925.

Kaga was also cancelled under the treaty, but before she could be broken up, Japan was struck by an earthquake which severely damaged the battlecruiser *Amagi*, scheduled for conversion into an aircraft carrier, and the decision was made to rebuild *Kaga* instead.

The carrier *Kaga* participated in the attack on Pearl Harbor on December 7, 1941, and also in naval operations against Rabaul and Port Darwin in 1942. She was sunk at the Battle of Midway on June 5, 1942.

The Japanese Navy had a tradition of innovation in battleship design, and many proposals were equal to, and sometimes better than, their foreign contemporaries. When *Nagato* was commissioned in the 1920s and *Yamato* in 1941 they were each in their time the world's most powerful battleship. In the 1920s a class of four fast battleships was planned which would have been about 50,000 tonnes/tons and armed with 450mm/18in guns, but these ships were cancelled under the Washington Treaty.

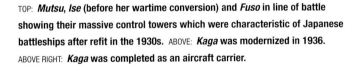

TOP: ***Mutsu**, **Ise** (before her wartime conversion) and **Fuso** in line of battle showing their massive control towers which were characteristic of Japanese battleships after refit in the 1930s.* ABOVE: ***Kaga** was modernized in 1936.* ABOVE RIGHT: ***Kaga** was completed as an aircraft carrier.*

Also a class of large cruisers, like the USN Alaska class, with 150mm/12in or 360mm/14in-guns was envisaged. The Japanese navy had an astonishing ability to redesign and rebuild capitals ships, even given the shortage of raw materials which was the *causus belli* of the attack on Pearl Harbor and the war in the Pacific. During the war resources were shifted from battleships to aircraft carriers, though it was a shortage of experienced pilots as much as any material or technological failure which brought about Japan's defeat.

Kaga class

Class: *Kaga, Tosa*. Launched 1921
Dimensions: Length – 231.5m/760ft
    Beam – 30.5m/100ft
    Draught – 10m/33ft 1in
Displacement: 40,540 tonnes/39,900 tons
Armament: Main – 10 x 405mm/16in guns
    Secondary – 20 x 140mm/5.5in,
    4 x 80mm/3.1in guns and
    8 x 610mm/24in torpedoes
Machinery: 12 oil and 4 mixed-fired boilers, 4
    shafts. 67,859kW/91,000shp
Speed: 26.5 knots
Complement: 1,333 men

Yamato class

Japanese war plans were for a pre-emptive strike which would sweep aside the weak opposition of the British, Dutch and French forces (who in the event were preoccupied with the war in Europe), to capture Wake and Guam, and to build and defend a perimeter around a zone of co-prosperity ruled by Japan. The Japanese wanted a quick peace with the USA, but if this was not going to be possible they reckoned that, with the USN exhausted and having suffered attrition during its passage across the Pacific, the Imperial Japanese Navy could meet the USN in a decisive battle close to its home base and annihilate it.

The Japanese navy studied Tsushima and Jutland but not the U-boat campaign of World War I. Little attention was paid to the convoying of Japanese merchant ships or to the attack upon shipping on America's long, vulnerable supply lines, and no plans were made for a long or defensive war. Furthermore, despite the success of carrier aviation at Pearl Harbor, they did not foresee the influence which carrier-borne aircraft would have on the war in the Pacific or have sufficient reserves of aircraft and pilots.

Nevertheless, the plan worked at first, although the attack on Pearl Harbor was counterproductive. Tactically it was a failure because the USN carriers were at sea and escaped

ABOVE: *Yamato,* **fitting out at Kure in September 1941, is seen here with her huge 455mm/18in guns in place. Japanese shipbuilding facilities had not progressed as much as their ship design and completion of the Yamato class to this stage was a considerable feat of ingenuity and logistics.**

damage. Politically it brought the USA into the war on the side of Britain, and it underestimated the strength of American rage and resolve. Industrially Japan could not match the unprecedented American construction programmes which turned out ships and aircraft and trained men at extraordinary rates. When by the end of 1942 Japanese and American naval losses were about the same (two battleships and four large aircraft carriers), the USN could have been expected to replace their ships whereas the Imperial Japanese Navy, which was already suffering shortages when the war started, could not compete despite desperate efforts.

However, if Japanese plans to consolidate and defend an area of influence in the Far East were to have any chance of success, a navy was needed superior to any rival, and this included the USN. When the Geneva Disarmament Conference broke down, Japan announced its intention to withdraw from the 1922 and 1930 naval treaties when they expired in 1936 and planning started on the giant battleships of the Yamato

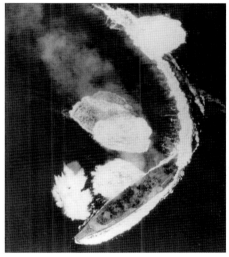

LEFT: *Yamato's* death throes after being attacked by USN aircraft in the East China Sea in April 1945. BELOW LEFT: *Yamato* at speed in December 1941. BELOW: *Yamato* manoeuvring to avoid air attack. By the end of the war USN fliers had been trained in huge numbers, and had the confidence of experience and superior aircraft, so that the Japanese surface fleet was no match for US naval aviation.

class. These ships were built in great secrecy, not excepting a 360-tonne/400-ton camouflage net to cover *Musashi* who at over 31,750 tonnes/35,000 tons was the largest ship to date launched from a slipway. *Yamato* and *Shinano* were built in new or specially enlarged docks, and a purpose-built heavy lift ship was needed to bring the guns and mountings to the shipyard. They were the largest battleships ever built, with the largest guns. Each mounting weighed over 2,270 tonnes/2,500 tons, and their range, at 45 degrees elevation, was 42,940m/ 46,960yd or 23 nautical miles. Their armour was supposed to give protection against 455mm/18in shells or a bomb dropped from 4,575m/15,000ft. The armoured belt was inclined at 20 degrees and below it was an inclined anti-torpedo belt: the weight and thickness of armour was impressive, though trials showed that the connection between the two belts was weak and the bulkheads were insufficiently elastic.

After many tank tests and competitive designs, there was an element of provocation in the final choice: it was reckoned that the largest ship which could pass through the Panama Canal was about 57,000 tonnes/63,000 tons, so if the USN was to out-build the Imperial Japanese Navy it would have to forgo the advantage of being able to swing its ships between the Atlantic and the Pacific, or widen the canal.

Yamato, the name ship of the class, was built at Kure naval dockyard. Commissioned in December 1941, just over a week after the start of the Pacific war, *Yamato* served as flagship of the Japanese Combined Fleet at the critical battles of 1942, including the Battle of Midway. This battle however was fought between the carrier groups; the battleships of the Japanese main force did not come into action and indeed the opposing fleets never saw each other.

She spent most of 1943 based at Truk and on December 24, 1943, was torpedoed by the American submarine *Skate,* requiring repairs which lasted until April 1944.

Like other Japanese and American battleships of the period, *Yamato*'s anti-aircraft battery was hugely increased before she took part in the Battle of the Philippine Sea in June. Again this was a carrier battle, in which Japanese naval air power was annihilated, and the battleships did not come into action and retreated upon Okinawa.

Yamato class (continued)

At the Battle of Leyte Gulf in October 1944 *Yamato* was part of the Japanese Centre Force, four surviving battleships and eight cruisers, which despite losing *Yamato*'s sister ship, *Mushashi*, in the Sibuyan Sea, pressed on into the actual Gulf on October 25. She helped to sink the escort carrier *Gambier Bay* and three destroyers by gunfire. The Centre Force was attacked several times by USN aircraft off the island of Samar, and just when it seemed the invasion forces must be destroyed, the Japanese admiral lost his nerve and retreated back through the San Bernardino Strait.

Yamato received little damage during the Battle of Leyte Gulf, and in Japan in November 1944 was fitted with yet more anti-aircraft guns. She was attacked by USN carrier planes in March 1945, and again slightly damaged. In April she took part in the suicidal Operation Ten-Go, intended to ruin the American invasion of Okinawa. On April 7, 1945, in the Battle of the East China Sea, some 320km/200 miles north of Okinawa, *Yamato* was attacked by a massive force of carrier planes from the USN Fifth Fleet and sunk.

Yamato's remains were located in 1985: she lies split in two at a depth of 305m/1,000ft. Her bows from B turret forward are upright, but the rest is upside down with a large hole close to the after magazines.

Musashi, sister ship of *Yamato*, was built at Nagasaki and commissioned in August 1942. The Japanese still conceived a decisive battle with the main fleet of the USN and in 1943 and 1944 *Musashi* was based at Truk to cover the threat of an American advance. Later she moved to Palau and on March 29, 1944, was torpedoed by the American submarine *Tunny*, needing repairs in Japan. *Musashi*'s anti-aircraft firepower was increased and in June 1944 she took part in the Battle of the Philippine Sea. Her last battle was during the Leyte Gulf campaign. *Musashi* was one of five battleships which formed the Centre Strike Force which, without carrier air support, intended to destroy the American landings on the Pacific coast of Leyte. On October 24, 1944, approaching from the west through the archipelagic Sibuyan Sea, and south of Luzon, *Musashi* and her consorts were attacked by American carrier aircraft. She was hit by 19 torpedoes and 17 bombs and though her armour enabled her to withstand more damage than any other ship might have done, several hours after the last attack she capsized and sank.

BELOW: ***Musashi*** caught leaving Brunei in October 1944, on what was to be the last major coordinated sortie by the Imperial Japanese Navy. Without aircraft carriers and naval air power to protect her, *Musashi* and her sisters were doomed.

Construction on *Shinano* as a battleship was stopped in 1942, and instead she was completed as an aircraft carrier in late 1944. However, while on trials, she was torpedoed and sunk by the American submarine *Archerfish* on November 29, 1944, as the USN blockade of Japanese waters increased.

Hull number 111 was intended to be a fourth Yamato class but construction on her was suspended in 1941 because of a shortage of skilled labour and materials, and cancelled in 1942; parts were used in three other ships.

Prior to World War II the Imperial Japanese Navy drew up plans for heavy cruisers or battlecruisers which would have been similar to the American Alaska class, and for a class of super-Yamatos, but all these plans were dropped for an emergency construction programme of aircraft carriers.

Yamato class

Class: *Yamato, Musashi, Shinano*, No. 111. Launched 1940–4

Dimensions: Length – 256m/839ft 9in
Beam – 37m/121ft
Draught – 10.5m/34ft

Displacement: 63,315 tonnes/62,315 tons

Armament: Main – 9 x 455mm/18in guns
Secondary – 12 x 155mm/6.1in,
12 x 125mm/5in and 24 x 25mm/1in guns

Machinery: 12 boilers, 4 shafts.
111,855kW/150,000shp

Speed: 27 knots

Complement: 2,500 men

LEFT: *Musashi* under air attack in the Sibuyan Sea. Cloud off the mountains and blue sky contrast sharply with death from the skies. BELOW: The Emperor Hirohito with officers of the battleship *Musashi* in 1943. Not even an emperor's support could help his navy once the USN had begun to exact its revenge for Pearl Harbor.

LEFT: **The so-called "pocket battleships" proved to be useful commerce raiders and tied up many British resources in the early months of World War II, but by mid-1942 they were either sunk or blockaded.** BELOW LEFT: *Admiral Graf Spee* **on launch. Launches of ships for the new German navy became opportunities for parade and display by the Nazi party.**

Deutschland (*Lützow*) and *Admiral Scheer*

The Treaty of Versailles which ended World War I imposed a displacement restriction on German warships of 10,160 tonnes/10,000 tons. In the 1920s the German navy tried to design an effective capital ship within this limit, varying the armament, armour, length and beam. The possibility of a heavy monitor for coastal defence or a large cruiser were examined and rejected, and eventually the design of a pocket battleship emerged. Weight was saved by using an all-welded construction, and the use of diesel engines gave good range and relatively high speed. The resulting ships were more powerful than any cruiser and faster than any battleship but there was no operational concept which justified these ships: the design was a matter of political and technical compromise. They were, however, well suited for commerce raiding.

Deutschland led an eventful life and survived World War II despite being frequently damaged, including being bombed by Republican aircraft off Ibiza on May 29, 1937, during the Spanish Civil War. *Deutschland* sailed prior to the outbreak of

World War II to a station off Greenland, where she sank two small ships and took another prize, and returned to the Baltic in mid-November, being renamed *Lützow* while still at sea. She took part in the German invasion of Norway, where she was hit by Norwegian coastal batteries on entering Oslo Fjord.

Whilst returning to Germany for repairs she was torpedoed by the British submarine *Spearfish* on April 11, 1940, and severely damaged. Later, while still under repair at Kiel, she was hit by a bomb which failed to explode during a raid by the Royal Air Force.

Then on June 13, 1941, *Lützow* was hit by an air-launched torpedo while en route to Norway, requiring her to return to Kiel for more repairs the next day. She eventually returned to Norway in May 1942, but ran aground and underwent more repairs in Germany. However, in December 1942 *Lützow*, the cruiser *Hipper* and their escorts attacked convoy JW51B off Bear Island and were driven off by a much weaker British squadron. When Hitler learned this he raged for an hour and a half on the theme that capital ships were a waste of men and material, during which time Grand Admiral Raeder "rarely had the opportunity to comment". The subsequent order to draw up plans for decommissioning the German big ships was a turning point in the war for the German navy and Raeder resigned after 14 years in office.

During 1943–5 *Lützow* was used in the Baltic, bombarding the seaward flank of the Soviet army, where on April 16, 1945, *Lützow* was badly damaged during an RAF bombing raid and she settled on the bottom. Her crew fought her as a fixed battery, firing on the advancing Soviet forces, until they blew her up on May 4, 1945. She was salvaged by the Russians and broken up in 1948–9.

Deutschland class

Class: *Deutschland, Admiral Scheer, Admiral Graf Spee*. Launched 1931–4

Dimensions: Length – 186m/610ft 3in
Beam – 21.6m/70ft 10in
Draught – 5.8m/19ft

Displacement: 11,890 tonnes/11,700 tons

Armament: Main – 6 x 280mm/11in guns
Secondary – 8 x 150mm/6in,
6 x 105mm/4.13in, 8 x 37mm/1.46in,
6 x 20mm/0.79in guns and
8 x 535mm/21in torpedoes

Machinery: 8 diesels, 3 shafts.
40,268kW/54,000hp

Speed: 28 knots

Complement: 619–1,150 men

Deutschland was renamed *Lützow* in 1939. Two more ships of the Deutschland class, as well as *Admiral Scheer* and *Admiral Graf Spee* (see over) were started but their material was used to build *Scharnhorst* and *Gneisenau*.

ABOVE LEFT: **Originally launched as *Deutschland*, Hitler later ordered her name to be changed to *Lützow* because he feared the loss of a ship with such a talismanic name.** LEFT: **A detail of *Deutschland* when newly completed, and being admired by onlookers.** BELOW: **Seamen of *Deutschland* receiving training in traditional skills in this photograph dated 1935. Oared craft were retained throughout the 20th century by all navies.**

Like *Deutschland*, *Admiral Scheer* saw service off Spain, and bombarded Almeria on May 31, 1937, in retaliation for the bombing of *Deutschland*. On September 4, 1939, *Admiral Scheer* was bombed in the Schillig Roads; she was also bombed on July 20, 1940, and again escaped damage. In October 1940 *Admiral Scheer* broke out into the North Atlantic where she was attacked by the armed merchant cruiser *Jervis Bay*. *Jervis Bay* was lost together with five ships of convoy HX84, but the remainder of the convoy scattered. *Admiral Scheer* then raided in the Atlantic and Indian Oceans, sinking 16 ships totalling 100,644 million tonnes/99,059 million tons until she returned, undetected, to Kiel on April 1, 1941.

In the summer of 1942 *Admiral Scheer* was part of the threatening fleet of German surface ships that sortied briefly during the debacle of convoy PQ17. She made one more sortie, sinking the Soviet icebreaker *Sibirjakov* on August 26, 1942, and bombarding the Russian coast, before going into a prolonged refit in November 1942. From November 1944 to March 1945 she was employed in coastal operations in the Baltic against the advancing Soviet army. Her luck finally ran out on April 9, 1945, when she was bombed and capsized. She was broken up *in situ,* 1948.

Admiral Graf Spee

Like her sisters, *Admiral Graf Spee* saw limited action off the coast of Spain during the Spanish Civil War. She sailed from Germany on August 21, 1939, to take up her station in the South Atlantic where together with her forays into the Indian Ocean she sank nine ships of 50,893 tonnes/50,089 tons. More than 20 British and French warships in eight groups were formed, each reckoned to be sufficient to despatch any raider of the pocket battleship type, and battleships and cruisers were deployed to act as escorts to ocean-going convoys in the North Atlantic. Thus, one objective of the German raider policy, to scatter and tie down enemy naval forces, was achieved.

The hunting groups were ordered to keep radio silence, which meant the Admiralty in London would not necessarily know about their movements, although they were ordered not to stray very far from concentrations of merchant ships. The Admiralty's orders foresaw that local commanders would need rather more than usual latitude to disregard any order they received, and to use their initiative.

At dawn on December 13, 1939, Force G under Commodore Henry Harwood found the *Admiral Graf Spee* off the River Plate. The battle which followed showed that the Royal Navy had learned a great deal since Jutland. After meeting his

captains in "Nelson style" onboard his flagship, Harwood gave his orders on the eve of battle in crisp sentences: "My policy with three cruisers in company versus one pocket battleship. Attack at once by day or night. By day act in two divisions ... by night ships will normally remain in company in open order." The three cruisers, the British 205mm/8in-gun cruiser *Exeter*

BELOW: *Admiral Graf Spee* attended the British Coronation Fleet Review at Spithead in 1937. Two years later, if *Admiral Graf Spee* had been flying her aircraft for dawn reconnaissance off the River Plate in December 1939, she might have avoided the searching British cruisers. RIGHT: On launch at Wilhelmshaven on June 30, 1934.

and the 150mm/6in-gun cruisers *Ajax* and the New Zealand *Achilles* had not operated together before, yet the following morning, no further tactical orders were necessary as the ships split into two divisions to divide the fire of their superior enemy.

Although *Exeter* in particular took terrible punishment from *Graf Spee*'s 280mm/11in guns, she did not blow up, as some of the battlecruisers at Jutland had done: the Royal Navy had clearly re-learned some key lessons about damage control and ammunition handling.

Exeter attacked from the south while the two light cruisers, *Ajax* and *Achilles*, worked around to the north acting as one division. *Admiral Graf Spee* concentrated her heavy armament on *Exeter*, putting her two after turrets out of action and forcing her to retire to the Falklands for repairs, while the two light cruisers dodged in and out of range of *Admiral Graf Spee*'s guns. *Admiral Graf Spee* does not seem to have been well handled and by 08.00, with only superficial damage, she broke off action and headed for the neutral port of Montevideo in Uruguay. She entered Montevideo at midnight with the two light cruisers hard on her heels, and there by diplomatic means she was maintained for several days while other British hunting groups headed for the area. By December 17 the only reinforcement which had arrived was the heavy cruiser *Cumberland* who, whilst refitting at the Falklands, had by a quirk of radio propagation heard the gunnery control signals and correctly interpreted that her presence was needed.

However, Langsdorff, the captain of the *Admiral Graf Spee*, had convinced himself that the entire Royal Navy was waiting for him and, having landed his crew, he scuttled his ship off Montevideo and committed suicide. His funeral was attended by some of the British merchant seamen he had held captive.

TOP: *Admiral Graf Spee* had a relatively low silhouette and consequently her secondary range-finder lacked height.
ABOVE: Photographed at Montevideo where she had taken refuge after the Battle of the River Plate, *Admiral Graf Spee* does not show much sign of damage. LEFT: *Admiral Graf Spee* was scuttled because her captain feared the arrival of British reinforcements to the cruisers who had driven him into port.

Scharnhorst and *Gneisenau*

TOP: **The Germans designed elegant and powerful-looking ships such as *Scharnhorst*.** ABOVE: ***Scharnhorst*'s sister ship *Gneisenau*.**

The original requirement for these two ships was that they should have the same speed and armament as the Deutschland class pocket battleships, but on a larger displacement – 19,305 tonnes/19,000 tons, allowing for heavier armour. The German navy's view was that if such a vessel was limited to 280mm/11in guns, then they should have a third triple turret, making the displacement 26,415 tonnes/26,000 tons. Hitler rejected this because he still did not want to break the Versailles Treaty and so provoke Britain. However, the Anglo-German Naval Agreement of 1935 allowed for two *panzerschiffe* of 26,415 tonnes/26,000 tons each armed with 280mm/11in guns. The agreement also allowed a maximum calibre of 406mm/16in and Hitler ordered the ships to be built with 380mm/15in guns, but the 280mm/11in triple turrets were available and it would have taken some time to develop a new turret. These new turrets were fitted to *Bismarck* and *Tirpitz* and although it was intended to up-gun *Scharnhorst* and *Gneisenau*, war prevented this. Both ships were refitted with the clipper or Atlantic bow on the eve of World War II, and during the war the close-range armament was increased. Two catapults were fitted, one high over the boat deck and the other on the roof of C turret which was removed pre-war.

Scharnhorst sank the armed merchant cruiser *Rawalpindi* in November 1939 but her planned breakout into the Atlantic was thwarted. On April 9, 1940, during the invasion of Norway she fought a brief battle with the battleship *Renown* but escaped in a snowstorm. On June 8, she sank the carrier *Glorious* and two destroyers, but the *Acasta* managed a torpedo hit which opened a large hole and flooded her. She was attacked by carrier-borne aircraft but escaped again to Kiel for repairs. In January 1942 *Scharnhorst* succeeded in breaking out into the Atlantic and sank several ships. She was hunted by British battleships but eluded them and reached Brest safely on March 23, 1942, after 60 days at sea and steaming 28,950km/18,000 miles. She was under repair for most of 1943 but in September she bombarded Spitsbergen and in December sallied to attack the Russia-bound convoy JW55B, when on December 26, 1943, she was overwhelmed by the

Scharnhorst class

Class: *Scharnhorst, Gneisenau.* Launched 1936
Dimensions: Length – 235m/770ft 8in
  Beam – 30m/98ft
  Draught – 8m/27ft
Displacement: 35,400 tonnes/34,841 tons
Armament: Main – 9 x 280mm/11in guns
  Secondary – 12 x 150mm/6in,
  14 x 105mm/4.13in, 16 x 37mm/1.46in and
  8 x 20mm/0.79in guns
Machinery: 12 boilers, 3 shafts.
  123,041kW/165,000shp
Speed: 32 knots
Complement: 1,669 men

TOP: *Scharnhorst* **firing her main armament.** TOP RIGHT: **A view of one of the** *schlachtschiff* **(battleship)** *Gneisenau's* **machinery rooms.** ABOVE: **Captain Ciliax, then commanding** *Scharnhorst,* **inspecting his ship's company pre-war. During the war he would make his fame in a German squadron, including leading these two ships, on the Channel Dash.**

battleship *Duke of York* and the cruisers *Belfast*, *Jamaica* and *Norfolk* and sunk with heavy loss of life.

For much of the war *Gneisenau* operated with *Scharnhorst*. However, on June 20, 1940, she was torpedoed by the submarine *Clyde* and only at the end of the year returned to Kiel for repairs. She broke out into the Atlantic with *Scharnhorst* in January to March 1942, and while in Brest was bombed many times, without serious damage. After being bombed by the RAF in November 1942 *Gneisenau* was taken in hand for the long-anticipated up-gunning. However, work was stopped in early 1943 and her armament used ashore. Three 280mm/11in guns were installed near the Hook of Holland and six in Norway. She was finally scuttled at Gdynia in 1945 and broken up between 1947 and 1951.

Scharnhorst and *Gneisenau* are best known for their Channel Dash or Operation Cerberus. Hitler was convinced that the British were going to invade Norway and personally ordered the Ugly Sisters, as the RAF knew them, home. Taking advantage of foul weather in the English Channel and by a combination of good luck and British failures, the Germans sailed on February 12, 1943, and evaded notice until they were about to enter the Straits of Dover. It was a bad day for the British, relieved only by the incredible bravery of the men of 825 Naval Air Squadron, led by Lieutenant Commander Eugene Esmonde, who was awarded a posthumous VC, for a "forlorn hope" attack in their *Swordfish*.

The dash by German warships up the English Channel was a humiliation for the British. *Scharnhorst* twice hit mines, and *Gneisenau* escaped only to be bombed at Kiel. A serious threat to allied shipping in the Atlantic was over and the German naval commander, Raeder, recognized that he had won a tactical victory but suffered a strategic defeat. The British could now concentrate their efforts against the German surface fleet, whose threat to shipping in the Atlantic had been diminished.

Bismarck

Design work on Germany's first fully-fledged battleships, with armament and armour equivalent to foreign capital ships, began in the early 1930s. Initially this class was supposed to be of 35,560 tonnes/35,000 tons displacement but the design was modified several times, even on the slipway, and after the Anglo-German naval treaty it was recognized that their standard displacement would be nearer 45,200 tonnes/45,000 tons, and eventually their deep load displacement exceeded 50,800 tonnes/50,000 tons.

The actual design was conservative, a development of World War I Baden design, with a main armament of eight 380mm/15in guns in twin turrets, two forward and two aft. Her secondary battery of six twin-turreted 150mm/6in guns were intended for use against destroyers, and her mixed anti-aircraft battery included guns of three different sizes: 105mm/4.1in, 37mm/1.46in and 20mm/0.79in was regarded as inadequate for World War II, given the developments there had been in naval aviation.

Bismarck was, however, very heavily armoured, again along the lines of the Baden class, and her broad beam gave her stability and made her a good, steady gun platform. Her 30-knot speed made for a fast battleship, but the steam plant was fuel-hungry and thus limited range, a defect which the German navy hoped to overcome by fitting diesel engines in all future designs. *Bismarck*'s keel was laid down in July 1936 and even after launch modifications continued, which took two years and included the fitting of a new clipper or Atlantic bow. As a result she was not ready until late in 1940.

ABOVE: *Bismarck* was hit by *Prince of Wales* during their brief battle on May 24, 1941, causing flooding forward which slowed the German ship down. She is seen here from *Prinz Eugen*, shortly before *Bismarck* feinted to the north to allow *Prinz Eugen* to escape. The Royal Navy thought, temporarily, that *Bismarck* was making back towards Norway, but soon resumed the chase to the south. Next, *Bismarck* was attacked from the air.

Germany naval strategy was to avoid set-piece battles with the Royal Navy and to conduct a war on commerce, using surface raiders, both warships and disguised merchant ships, and U-boats. The intention was both to disperse British forces, to force merchant ships into inefficient convoys and then to disrupt the convoy patterns, as well as to destroy shipping. Under this plan battleships and cruisers were to evade the British blockade and break out into the Atlantic, and eventually the Indian and Pacific Oceans. The heavy cruisers *Admiral Hipper* and *Prinz Eugen*, the pocket battleships *Lützow*, *Admiral Graf Spee* and *Admiral Scheer*, the battlecruisers *Scharnhorst* and *Gneisenau*, and, of course, *Bismarck* were faster than most British battleships. This posed a serious threat which was taken very seriously by the Royal Navy and also by the French navy while it was still active in World War II. Germany's strategy was not successful while her navy could be blockaded in the North Sea, but after the fall of France in June 1940, when the German fleet had access to the French Atlantic ports, the strategic balance changed. In December 1940 and early 1941 German surface raiders sank 47 merchant ships, and U-boats sank many more.

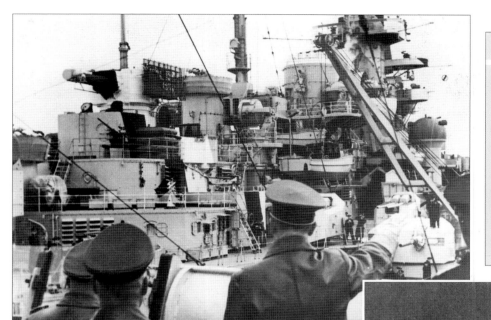

Bismarck

Class: *Bismarck, Tirpitz.* Launched 1939
Dimensions: Length – 248m/813ft 8in
    Beam – 36m/118ft 1in
    Draught – 8.5m/28ft 6in
Displacement: 42,370 tonnes/41,700 tons
Armament: Main – 8 x 380mm/15in guns
    Secondary – 12 x 150mm/6in,
    16 x 105mm/4.13in, 16 x 37mm/1.46in and
    12 x 20mm/0.79in guns
Machinery: 12 boilers, 3 shafts.
    102,907kW/138,000shp
Speed: 29 knots
Complement: 2,092–2,608 men

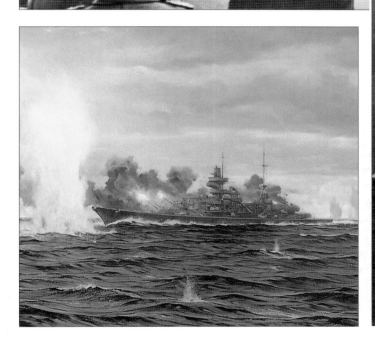

TOP: **Hitler making the Nazi salute towards *Bismarck*, though oddly there does not seem to be anyone on the upper deck to return the compliment.** ABOVE : ***Bismarck* was finally overwhelmed by the British Home Fleet.** ABOVE RIGHT: ***Bismarck* photographed from *Prinz Eugen* during the encounter with *Hood*.**

In May 1941 the German navy sent *Bismarck* and the heavy cruiser *Prinz Eugen* on a raid into the Atlantic. The movement was spotted but in bad weather the Germans got into the Denmark Strait, where they were shadowed by two British cruisers. On May 24, 1941, during a brief battle between the two Germans and the British *Prince of Wales* and *Hood*, *Hood* blew up and *Prince of Wales* was damaged. *Bismarck* however was hit by 355mm/14in shells from *Prince of Wales* which caused her to lose fuel and contaminated several bunkers with salt water. *Prinz Eugen* was detached into the Atlantic while *Bismarck* headed for Brest. Next, presaging the new relationship between battleship and aircraft which would change naval warfare forever, a strike by nine aircraft from the aircraft carrier *Victorious* hit *Bismarck* with one torpedo, but the damage was slight.

For two days *Bismarck* escaped detection while the hunting British fleet cast to the north, thinking that *Bismarck* might have been returning to Norway. However, she was spotted by the American pilot of a RAF flying boat and in the evening of May 26, and in appalling weather, the aircraft of the carrier *Ark Royal* crippled *Bismarck* by wrecking her steering gear and jamming her rudder. At dawn the next day the battleships *King George V* and *Rodney* opened fire on the German ship at a range of 14,630m/16,000yds, and in an hour and a half *Bismarck* was reduced to a blazing wreck. She was torpedoed and sank some 555km/300 nautical miles west of Ushant. Of her crew of 2,222 men only 110 survived the sinking.

Tirpitz

The sister ship of *Bismarck*, *Tirpitz* was commissioned in February 1941, when she operated in the Baltic on trials and training, and was engaged in support of Operation Barbarossa, the German advance into Russia. However, in January 1942 *Tirpitz* was sent to Norway: Hitler was obsessed that "the fate of the war will be decided in Norway", and throughout the war kept large forces there. Here *Tirpitz* acted like a fleet-in-being and in turn consumed British effort and imagination in plans for her destruction.

One of *Tirpitz*'s few offensive actions was Operation Rösselsprung or "knight's move", a planned attack on convoy traffic in June and July 1942. It was spoilt when three destroyers escorting the German Battle Group I, consisting of *Tirpitz* and the heavy cruiser *Admiral Hipper*, grounded outside Altenfjord. The pocket battleship *Lützow*, belonging with *Admiral Scheer* to Battle Group II, was also stranded and needed repairs in Germany. Both battle groups turned back when the Germans suspected an attack by submarines and carrier aircraft. However, when the British Admiralty dispersed the convoy PQ17, 19 of the 36 merchant ships were subsequently lost to German aircraft or U-boats.

At the end of 1942 there was a failed attempt to attack *Tirpitz* at her anchorage by miniature submarines and two-man torpedoes known as chariots, carried into the fjords by a Norwegian fishing boat. The bombing of *Gneisenau* showed that it was unsafe for *Tirpitz* to return to Germany and so she was refitted in the fjords, where in March 1943 she was joined by *Prinz Eugen*, *Scharnhorst* and *Lützow*. On September 8, 1943, *Tirpitz* and *Scharnhorst* bombarded Spitsbergen, which was to be the last time *Tirpitz* fired her main armament in anger.

Back in Kaafjord, the Royal Navy mounted Operation Source in September 1943, an attack using X-craft towed into position by parent submarines. Shortly after 08.00 on September 21, two violent explosions underneath *Tirpitz* forced her upwards several feet. All power was lost and she settled with a list to port. The damage was severe: there were splits in the bottom of the hull, buckling and distortion; a generator room was flooded and electrical generators lifted off their mountings; the propeller shafts were jammed and A and X turrets jumped off their roller paths.

BELOW: *Tirpitz* **underway for her sea trials in 1941. Her sister ship** *Bismarck* **had a career which could be measured in months.** *Tirpitz*'**s career lasted only a handful of years and she saw little action, although her presence as fleet-in-being in a lair in a Norwegian fjord and the threat she represented, in particular to Arctic convoys to Russia, tied up huge resources.**

ABOVE: **Hitler inspecting the parade before the launch of** *Tirpitz* **on April 1, 1939. Top left is the hull of** *Tirpitz* **showing the bilge keel which ran each side of the length of the ship.** TOP RIGHT: *Tirpitz* **in her lair with smokescreens put up to obscure her from the air during attack by the Fleet Air Arm.** RIGHT: **Sunk at last after several raids,** *Tirpitz* **turned turtle and was scrapped** *in situ***, by a Norwegian company. Some portions of her still lie on the bottom of the fjord in her last berth.**

During the winter of 1943–4 the Germans repaired *Tirpitz*, who, despite receiving further shock damage by Soviet bombers in February, was able to begin manoeuvring trials in the following spring. There then began a series of attacks by carrier aircraft of the Royal Navy.

The first of these, Operation Tungsten, comprised the battleships *Duke of York* and *Anson*, the carriers *Victorious*, *Furious*, *Searcher*, *Pursuer* and *Emperor* and a large number of cruisers and destroyers. Fleet Air Arm Barracuda torpedo-bombers, Wildcats and Hellcats struck on April 3, 1944, just as *Tirpitz* was weighing anchor for post-repair trials. The first attack lasted barely a minute and scored six direct hits, and a second attack a few minutes later scored eight direct hits: there were other probable hits and the aircraft descended to strafe *Tirpitz* as well. By 08.00 all the aircraft but three had landed on their carriers.

Similar attacks were cancelled as a result of bad weather, but on July 17, 1944, Operation Mascot scored a near-miss despite improved anti-aircraft defences and *Tirpitz* was only saved from further damage by an effective smokescreen. Nevertheless, *Tirpitz*'s much-delayed sea trials on July 31 and August 1, 1944, were her last.

In August a series of operations all codenamed Goodwood using the carriers *Indefatigable*, *Formidable*, *Furious*, *Nabob* and *Trumpeter* started. Goodwood III on August 24, 1944, was the heaviest and most determined so far, and even the Germans admired the British skill and dexterity in flying. The effect of all these attacks was to render *Tirpitz* unserviceable from September 1943 onwards.

Finally, on September 15, 1944, 33 Lancaster bombers, which had been pre-positioned in Russia, attacked using 5,445kg/12,000lb bombs nicknamed Tallboys. By now the German anti-aircraft fire included a barge firing next to her 380mm/15in guns, but despite this one bomb hit *Tirpitz* and exploded underneath, flooding the forward part of the ship and shaking much of her machinery off its mountings. *Tirpitz* was towed to shallower water where on November 12 she was again attacked by Lancaster bombers dropping Tallboys. There were two direct hits and several near-misses and an internal explosion, whereupon *Tirpitz* rolled over to port and capsized with heavy loss of life.

Tirpitz was broken up *in situ* between 1949 and 1957 by a Norwegian company.

Tirpitz

Class: *Bismarck*, *Tirpitz*. Launched 1939
Dimensions: Length – 248m/813ft 8in
    Beam – 36m/118ft 1in
    Draught – 8.5m/28ft 6in
Displacement: 42,370 tonnes/41,700 tons
Armament: Main – 8 x 380mm/15in guns
    Secondary – 12 x 150mm/6in,
    16 x 105mm/4.13in, 16 x 37mm/1.46in and
    12 x 20mm/0.79in guns
Machinery: 12 boilers, 3 shafts.
    102,907kW/138,000shp
Speed: 29 knots
Complement: 2,092–2,608 men

LEFT: **A stern view of _Dunkerque_, showing the hangar for her aircraft – then quite an advanced feature of warship design.** ABOVE: **The French battleships _Strasbourg_ and _Dunkerque_ at their berth in Mers-el-Kebir in Algeria (then a French colony), where they had taken refuge after the fall of France. While at berth they were attacked by the Royal Navy in July 1940, after the French had refused British proposals to ensure that their fleet would not fall into the possession of the Nazis.**

Dunkerque and _Strasbourg_

These two ships, built as part of France's battleship tonnage allowed by the Washington Naval Treaty, were like the British Nelson class in having all of their main armament forward. France was allowed a total battleship displacement of 177,800 tonnes/175,000 tons under the treaty. Smaller and cheaper ships were sought, but the French navy eventually settled on a design of 26,925 tonnes/ 26,500 tons, partly in response to the heavy cruisers built in Germany and the new Italian battleships which were known to be in progress. The treaty allowed guns of up to 380mm/15in, but on grounds of economy France chose a new calibre of 330mm/13in.

Other novel features included a large number of medium-calibre and anti-aircraft guns in quadruple mountings and a purpose-built aircraft hangar aft. A prominent feature of these ships was a control tower consisting of three separate structures rotating on a common axis and weighing more than 86 tonnes/85 tons.

In 1939 _Dunkerque_ was part of Force I, one of several British and French forces formed to hunt down German raiders in the Atlantic and Indian Oceans. In December she carried French gold to Canada for safekeeping and returned escorting Canadian troop convoys to Britain. After the fall of France, she was badly damaged twice while alongside at Mers-el-Kebir, after senior French officers had refused British proposals to neutralize their fleet to prevent it being used by the Nazis. Consequently the Royal Navy bombarded the port on July 3 and British aircraft attacked on July 6 to stop French warships falling into Nazi hands. After emergency repairs she was taken to Toulon, where on November 27, 1942, she was sabotaged by loyal Frenchmen and stranded in her dry dock for the next three years. She was finally sold for scrap in 1956.

Strasbourg was also involved in the 1939 hunt for the German pocket battleship _Admiral Graf Spee_, which was raiding in the South Atlantic. She suffered a similar fate to _Dunkerque_: although only lightly damaged by British shelling at Mers-el-Kebir, she was scuttled by the French at Toulon on November 27, 1942, and despite attempts at salvage, was sunk again by US aircraft in August 1944 during Allied landings in the south of France. She was sold for scrap in 1955.

Dunkerque class

Class: _Dunkerque, Strasbourg._
    Launched 1935–6
Dimensions: Length – 214.5m/703ft 9in
    Beam – 31m/102ft
    Draught – 8.7m/28ft 6in
Displacement: 26,925 tonnes/26,500 tons
Armament: Main – 8 x 330mm/13in guns
    Secondary – 16 x 130mm/5.1in,
    8 x 37mm/1.46in and 32 x 13mm/0.52in guns
Machinery: 6 boilers, 4 shafts.
    83,891kW/112,500shp
Speed: 29.5 knots
Complement: 1,431 men

LEFT: *Richelieu* at Dakar in 1941. *Richelieu* exchanged shots with the British *Resolution*, and her sister ship *Jean Bart* exchanged shots with the USN *Massachusetts*. BELOW: *Richelieu*, having fought the British at Dakar, declared for the Free French, was refitted in New York and fought alongside the British in the Far East.

Richelieu class

After the Anglo-German naval agreement and the abrogation or expiry of the Washington Naval Treaty, France considered herself free to expand her navy. The Richelieu class represented a further development of the Dunkerque class, but was 10,160 tonnes/10,000 tons larger, with 380mm/15in guns, and a speed of 2 to 3 knots faster.

Richelieu and *Jean Bart* escaped from France. *Richelieu* benefited from being completed in New York and gaining from USN experience in the Pacific. *Jean Bart*, which carried very heavy anti-aircraft armament, was damaged during the Allied landings in North Africa and work to complete her did not recommence until 1946. A novel feature of the design included blowers to mix cold fresh air with the hot flue gases and so minimize the effect upon fire-control optics.

Before completion *Richelieu* was moved from Brest to Dakar, where on July 8, 1944, she was damaged by aircraft from the British carrier *Hermes* and again between September 23 and 25 during a duel with the battleship *Resolution*. Once taken over by the Free French navy she sailed for New York where she was finally completed, and in November 1943 began operations with

the British Home Fleet. In 1944 and 1945 she operated with the British East Indies Fleet and then the British Pacific Fleet, visiting Toulon in September 1944 and returning to Cherbourg in March 1946. She was broken up in Italy in 1968.

The incomplete *Jean Bart* escaped from St Nazaire and evaded the advancing Germans in June 1940, eventually reaching Casablanca. There, in November 1942 during Allied landings in North Africa, she exchanged fire with the USN battleship *Massachusetts* and received several gunfire and bomb hits. She was towed to Brest after the war and completed in 1955. *Jean Bart* took part in the Suez campaign in 1956, was decommissioned in the 1960s and scrapped in Japan in 1969.

Clémenceau was only 10 per cent complete when France was overrun by the Germans and she was declared war booty. The hull section was floated out of

dock but never worked on again and was sunk in a US air raid in 1944. *Gascogne* was never started.

A final class of battleships, *Alsace*, *Normandie*, *Flandre* and *Bourgogne* was proposed for 1940 onwards but not actually implemented.

Richelieu class

Class: *Richelieu, Jean Bart, Clémenceau, Gascogne.* Launched 1939–40
Dimensions: Length – 247.8m/813ft
  Beam – 33m/108ft 3in
  Draught – 9.65m/31ft 7in
Displacement: 35,560 tonnes/35,000 tons
Armament: Main – 8 x 380mm/15in guns
  Secondary – 9 x 150mm/6in, 12 x 99mm/3.9in,
  8 x 37mm/1.46in and 16 x 13mm/0.52in guns
Machinery: 6 boilers, 4 shafts.
  111,855kW/150,000shp
Speed: 32 knots
Complement: 1,670 men
Jean Bart was fitted with bulges and had a beam of 35.5m/116ft.

Conte di Cavour class

Class: *Conte di Cavour, Giulio Cesare, Leonardo da Vinci.* Launched 1911
Dimensions: Length – 186.1m/610ft 6in
Beam – 28m/91ft 10in
Draught – 9.3m/30ft 6in
Displacement: 24,405 tonnes/23,600 tons
Armament: Main – 10 x 320mm/12.6in guns
Secondary – 12 x 120mm/4.7in guns
Machinery: 8 boilers, 2 turbines.
65,859kW/93,000shp
Speed: 28 knots
Complement: 1,230 men
The specifications given here are for the ships as they were rebuilt in the 1930s.

LEFT: *Conte di Cavour* and *Guilio Cesare* were modernized in the 1930s. The reconstruction amounted to a complete rebuild which totally changed their profile, as well as adding 10.3m/34ft to their length.

Conte di Cavour class (1933)

Starting in 1933 *Conte di Cavour* and *Giulio Cesare* were completely rebuilt. A new bow section added more than 9m/30ft to their length. New oil-fired boilers and turbines driving two shafts, reduced from four, delivered three times more horsepower. This, with the longer hull ratio, produced 6 knots of extra speed. The midships turret was suppressed and the ships were given a completely new superstructure. The 305mm/12in main armament was replaced by 320mm/12.6in guns, and the armoured protection increased. Horizontal armour was increased to 135mm/5.3in and vertical armour around the turrets by an additional 50mm/1.97in. The Pugliese system was installed in which fuel tanks ran the length of the ship, and these contained a large empty cylinder intended as a shock absorber to minimize a hit on or below the waterline.

Conte di Cavour took part in the action off Punto Stilo on July 9, 1940, also known as the Battle of Calabria, when the British battleships *Malaya*, *Barham* and *Royal Sovereign* chased the Italian fleet to within sight of the coast of Calabria. Battles such as this helped to establish the superior morale of the British battlefleet under Cunningham's aggressive command. There followed other largely unsuccessful actions against the British fleet and various Malta convoys. On November 11, 1940, Swordfish torpedo-bombers from the British carrier *Illustrious* attacked the Italian fleet in the harbour of Taranto and *Conte di Cavour* was sunk by a torpedo. Raised and towed to Trieste for repairs, she was sunk again by the Italians to prevent her falling into German hands, only to be raised by the Germans but sunk again by the USAAF in 1945. She was scrapped in 1951.

Giulio Cesare was hit by a 380mm/15in-shell from the British *Warspite* during the Battle of Punto Stilo. She took part in the action near Cape Teulada in November 27, 1940, against Force H and the battleships *Renown* and *Ramillies*, and was engaged against British cruisers and destroyers at the First Battle of Sirte on December 17, 1941.

By early 1942 *Giulio Cesare* was reduced to the status of a training and barracks ship. Allocated to the Soviet Union as war reparations, she became the *Novorossijsk*, but was lost in 1955 as a result of striking a mine in the Black Sea.

Leonardo da Vinci was sunk by a magazine explosion in 1916, attributed (probably wrongly) to Austrian saboteurs. Although she was refloated and it was planned to refit the hull, she was scrapped in the 1920s.

Caio Duilio class (1937)

Like their near sisters, the Conte di Cavour class, these ships were completely rebuilt under Mussolini's regime in Italy. The hull was lengthened by inserting a new bow section, and they were given an all-new propulsion plant, driving two shafts. These measures together gave them 6 knots of extra speed, up to 27 knots. The midships turret was removed and they were given new superstructures. The main armament was increased to 320mm/ 12.6in calibre, the secondary armament of 12 135mm/5.3in guns was mounted in four triple turrets, and they also carried numerous lighter anti-aircraft guns. Armour was also increased and they received the Pugliese protection system.

Caio Duilio re-entered service in July 1940 and thereafter was involved in a number of unsuccessful skirmishes against the British Mediterranean Fleet. During the attack on Taranto by aircraft of the Royal Navy's Fleet Air Arm she received one torpedo hit but remained afloat and the following month was at sea on North Africa convoy duties. On December 17, 1941, she fought a brief and unsuccessful action with British cruisers and destroyers in what became known as the First Battle of Sirte. She was surrendered to the Royal Navy on September 9, 1943, when the Italian government signed an armistice with the Allies, and scrapped in 1957.

Andrea Doria was also unsuccessful against the British Mediterranean Fleet, although regularly employed on convoy protection duties to and from North Africa and in attempts to disrupt British convoys to Malta. She escaped damage during the British attack on Taranto harbour on November 11, but did join *Caio Duilio* in the unsuccessful action at the First Battle of Sirte. *Andrea Doria* was surrendered to the Royal Navy at Malta on September 9, 1943, and scrapped in 1957.

Caio Duilio class

Class: *Caio Duilio, Andrea Doria*. Launched 1913
Dimensions: Length – 186.9m/613ft 2in
  Beam – 28m/91ft 10in
  Draught – 9.5m/30ft 10in
Displacement: 21,590 tonnes/23,800 tons
Armament: Main – 10 x 320mm/12.6in guns
  Secondary – 12 x 135mm/5.3in,
Machinery: 8 boilers, 2 turbines.
  59,859kW/87,000shp
Speed: 27 knots
Complement: 1,490 men
The specifications given here are for the ships as they were rebuilt in the 1930s.

ABOVE: **Detail of the port quarter of *Andrea Doria*.** LEFT: **The Caio Duilio class and the Conte di Cavour class were similar ships when first built, with tall funnels, even taller tripod masts and a midships turret, as seen here. Contrast this with the 1930s rebuild opposite, which gave the ships of these two classes a much lower profile. The length was increased too and with more efficient machinery, which nearly tripled the horsepower, the speed was increased in both classes by some 6 knots. Improved armour increased displacement by some 2,032tonnes/2,000 tons.**

Vittorio Veneto class

These handsome battleships were the first to be built by Italy after the Washington Naval Treaty, and were partly a response to the French *Dunkerque* and *Strasbourg*. Clearly the Italians were intent upon breaching the treaty limit of 35,560 tonnes/35,000 tons, and at full load these ships displaced more than 45,720 tonnes/45,000 tons. The guns were 380mm/15in, rather than the 405mm/16in which were permitted by treaty, which was due to the limited capacity of the Italian ordnance industry. However they were long guns capable, in theory, of a range of 42,062m/46,000yds.

With the exception of the 120mm/4.7in guns which were old Armstrong weapons, all the guns were of a new design, and, given the environment in which these ships would operate, the anti-aircraft armament was increased during the war.

The armour which was up to 350mm/13.8in thick was intended to defeat 380mm/15in shells at 16,000m/17,500yds, and there was complex subdivision inside the hull, including the Pugliese system. This consisted of a torpedo bulkhead

ABOVE: **Italian design at its best, *Vittorio Veneto* was built in 1934–40 and scrapped in 1948–51.** BELOW LEFT: **The Vittorio Veneto class were beamy, well-thought-out ships intended for war in the Mediterranean. With its mix of new and modernized battleships and the ability to operate under the cover of aircraft from numerous shore airfields, the Italian navy had the material to dominate the Mediterranean. However, in early encounters Cunningham and his British Mediterranean Fleet established their superior morale.**

which curved inboard and downward to meet the outer bottom. Within this was a compartment containing an empty longitudinal drum which was manufactured under pressure thus absorbing the force of any explosion, however, poor construction technique was blamed for the system not proving as effective in action as was hoped.

As they often showed in battle with the British, this class of ship was capable of high sustained speed. A quarterdeck catapult could launch three reconnaissance planes or, as the war progressed, three fighters. In September 1941 *Littorio* became the first Italian battleship to be fitted with radar.

Vittorio Veneto was the busiest of the Italian battleships. Completed in April 1940, she escaped damage during the attack on Taranto, and was flagship of the Italian fleet during the Battle of Cape Matapan in March 1941. Here she was hit during a torpedo attack by *Formidable*'s aircraft, but was not slowed sufficiently to allow Cunningham in *Warspite* with the British Mediterranean Fleet to catch up. She then underwent repairs until August 1941. Her main employment was as distant cover for Axis Africa-bound convoys and the interdiction of British Malta-bound shipping. On November 8, 1941, the cruisers *Aurora* and *Penelope*, forming the British Force K, sallied from Malta and snapped up a convoy supposedly under the *Vittorio Veneto*'s protection. Then on December 14, 1941, the British submarine *Urge* torpedoed the *Vittorio Veneto* and she required repairs which lasted until early 1942. In June 1943

TOP: *Littorio* (formerly *Italia*) was badly damaged at Taranto in November 1940 by the British Fleet Air Arm. ABOVE: *Roma* on her launch in 1940.
LEFT: *Roma* having entered the war against the British was on her way to surrender at Malta when she was bombed by her erstwhile allies, the Germans, and sunk.

she was bombed while at La Spezia. After being surrendered to the British at Malta in September 1943, she was interned at Suez and then returned to Italy, being scrapped in 1948.

Littorio, as she is better known, was damaged in Taranto by three torpedoes delivered by Swordfish aircraft from the British carrier *Illustrious*. She sank by the bows and remained under repair at Taranto until August 1941. At the Second Battle of Sirte on March 22, 1942, she made a determined attempt to interdict a four-ship convoy protected by British cruisers and destroyers under the command of Admiral Philip Vian, but was driven off by superior tactics, including the use of smokescreens and torpedo attack. She was renamed *Italia* on July 30, 1943, after the overthrow of Mussolini, and was badly damaged on September 9, 1941, by German glider bombs but survived. After internment at Alexandria, she was returned to Italy in 1947 and scrapped.

Roma was bombed in La Spezia in June 1942 as she was nearing completion. Repaired, she sailed in September 1943 with the Italian fleet to its surrender under the guns of Malta, but was struck by a German glider bomb and sank with heavy losses. *Impero* was never completed and was taken over by

the Germans at the Italian armistice; she was bombed and sunk in Trieste in 1945, and scrapped in 1950. With the loss of all its battleships at the end of World War II, Italy's attempt to join the first rank of navies was brought to an end, despite leading some of the stages of battleship development and designing some very graceful ships.

Vittorio Veneto class

Class: *Vittorio Veneto, Italia* (ex *Littorio*), *Roma, Impero.* Launched 1937–40
Dimensions: Length – 224m/735ft
Beam – 32.75m/107ft 5in
Draught – 9.6m/31ft 5in
Displacement: 41,377 tonnes/40,724 tons
Armament: Main – 9 x 380mm/15in guns
Secondary – 12 x 155mm/6.1in,
4 x 120mm/4.7in, 12 x 90mm/3.54in,
20 x 37mm/1.46in and 16 x 20mm/0.79in guns
Machinery: 8 boilers, 4-shaft geared turbines.
96,940kW/130,000shp
Speed: 30 knots
Complement: 1,830–1,950 men

Sovyetskiy Soyuz class

Under the Soviet second five-year plan (1933–7) the old Imperial shipyards at Leningrad and Nikolayev were modernized. In 1938 the *Sovyetskiy Soyuz* was laid down at the Baltic shipyard, known in the Soviet era as the Ordzhonikidze Shipyard (No. 189), and *Sovyetskaya Ukraina* at the Andre Marti Shipyard (No. 198) at Nikolayev on the Black Sea. New yards were also built in the Arctic and the Far East, as well as inland on canals which could be used to take unfinished hulls to the coast for completion. One of the new yards was Shipyard No. 402 at Molotovsk (now Severodvinsk) on the White Sea, where the construction hall was big enough to take two super-battleships of the Sovyetskiy Soyuz class side by side.

After World War I, the Soviet Union was not regarded as a naval power and had not been invited to any of the inter-war naval arms conferences. Stalin apparently studied the strategic writings of the American naval officer, Mahan, who urged

nations (in his case the USA) to obtain a navy for geo-strategic purposes, and wanted a navy for the Soviet Union for reasons of self-esteem as much as for national security. The Soviet Union therefore became a late signatory of the London Naval Treaty and in 1937 signed a bilateral Anglo-Soviet Naval agreement. Stalin ordered his agents to purchase whatever was needed from his capitalist enemies for the Soviet naval programme, and they eventually obtained plans bought from Italy, who had supplied the Imperial Russian Navy, to help work up their own version of a super-Dreadnought. Blueprints were also purchased from the USA, despite objections from the USN, and in 1940 the Soviet navy sought help from Nazi Germany.

The initial Soviet plan was to build a fleet of 16 battleships and 12 heavy cruisers and corresponding numbers of other warships during the next two five-year plans. It is doubtful whether the Soviets ever had the technology to achieve this

LEFT: **Soviet plans to build battleships in the inter-war years came to nothing. However the Soviets did acquire the Italian *Giulio Cesare* as war reparation in 1948. Italian naval officers and men refused to steam *Giulio Cesare* to Russia, and so she had to be manned with a civilian crew.** BELOW: **The British also lent *Royal Sovereign* between 1944 and 1949, seen here flying the Soviet flag.**

Sovyetskiy Soyuz class

Class: *Sovyetskiy Soyuz, Sovyetskaya Ukraina, Sovyetskaya Byelorussiya, Sovyetskaya Rossiya.* Not launched.

Dimensions: Length – 271m/889ft
Beam – 38.7m/127ft
Draught – 10.1m/33ft 2in

Displacement: 60,099 tonnes/59,150 tons

Armament: Main – 9 x 405mm/16in guns
Secondary – 12 x 150mm/6in,
8 x 100mm/4in and 32 x 37mm/1.46in guns

Machinery: boilers, 3 shafts turbo-electric.
172,257kW/231,000shp

Speed: 28 knots

plan or any of its subsequent alterations and it certainly did not have the finance. However four Sovyetskiy Soyuz class battleships were authorized in 1938 and construction of three of them was started. All three were overtaken by war.

The design bore a passing resemblance to the Italian Vittorio Veneto class, with two triple turrets forward, B turret super-firing over A, and an after turret in a tall barbette. They also had a tall tower superstructure forward of two large upright funnels. The Italian Pugliese system of underwater protection was also adopted. None of these ships were completed, and all were broken up in the 1940s.

From May 1944 to February 1949 the Soviet navy was lent the British battleship *Royal Sovereign* under the name of *Arkhangelsk*, pending delivery of an equivalent Italian battleship as part of the Soviet Union's share of war reparations. She was used to escort Arctic convoys, but became something of a target for German U-boats, including an attack by Biber midget submarines, and spent much of the time behind anti-submarine nets. She was returned to Britain in 1949 and broken up.

As for the Sovyetskiy Soyuz class itself, these were by far the largest Russian warships designed, but the German invasion prevented their completion, and the post-war shipyards lacked the capacity and the political direction to continue to build battleships. The name ship of the class, *Sovyetskiy Soyuz*, was well advanced when war broke out, but between 1941 and 1944 most of the armour was removed for use elsewhere in the Soviet war economy. Post-war she was cut into sections and scrapped. Work on the second ship, *Sovyetskaya Ukraina*, was almost 75 per cent complete when the German army occupied Nikolayev on August 16, 1941. When the German army evacuated the city in 1944 they damaged the building slip and the ship, preventing her completion. No progress was made with the other two ships of the class, *Sovyetskaya Byelorussiya* and *Sovyetskaya Rossiya*.

By the end of World War II the Soviet navy still had not recovered from its parlous state after the Battle of Tsushima, and the world had to wait until the Cold War, when it briefly flourished under Admiral Gorshkov.

Glossary

aft
At or towards the rear or stern.

battle cruiser
Ship armed with battleship-sized guns, but in which armour has been dispensed with for speed and manoeuvrability.

beam
The widest part of a ship.

bilge
The lowest part of the hull of a ship, where the side turns into the bottom.

bilge keel
Fins or narrow wings at the turn of the bilge, designed to improve stability.

blister
See bulge.

block ship
A battleship converted into a floating battery intended to defend habours.

bow (or bows)
The forward end of a ship.

breastwork
Raised armoured bulkhead to protect a gun and its moving parts.

bulge (or blister)
A longitudinal space, subdivided and filled with fuel, water or air, to protect against the effects of a torpedo hit.

bulkhead
The internal vertical structures within a ship.

calibre
The internal diameter or bore of a gun, or the ratio of the barrel length to the bore.

capital ship
A generic name given to the largest and most powerful ships in a navy.

chariot
A two-manned torpedo used to attack enemy shipping in harbour.

cofferdam
Watertight bulkhead separating and protecting magazines and engine rooms.

dressed overall
A ship dressed *en fête*, flying lines of flags between her masts, when not underway.

dwarf bulkhead
Low bulkhead intended to stop the free flood of water.

flotilla
A squadron in the Royal Navy before NATO standardization.

flying deck
A deck suspended between two parts of the superstructure so that the deck below can be kept clear for mounting guns.

forecastle
Forward part of a ship.

freeboard
Height of the deck above the waterline.

gunwales
Upper edge of the side of a vessel.

heel
Lean or tilt of a ship.

ihp
Indicated horsepower: the calculated output of a ship's machinery.

laid down	Reference to when a new ship was first placed on the construction slip.
line ahead	When ships form up in a line.
line-of-battle ship	A ship large enough to be in the line.
metacentre	Roll and return to upright slowly.
monitor	Low freeboard coast defence vessel.
NATO	North Atlantic Treaty Organization.
ordnance	Armament and ammunition of a ship.
pole mast	A stick-like mast to carry aerials or flags.
pocket battleship	Small German battleship designed in the interwar years to circumvent restrictions on total tonnage and size.
pom pom	The name for a type of 1- or 2-pounder gun derived from the sound of its firing.
port	Left side.
quarter	Between the beam and the stern.
screw	Propeller.
shp	Shaft horse power: the actual measured output of a ship's machinery.
starboard	Right side.
stern	Rear of a ship.
theatre	The area in which a ship or fleet operates or a naval campaign takes place.
tripod mast	A mast having extra legs to carry the weight of direction-finding and gunnery control positions.
tumblehome	Inward curve of a ship's side above the waterline.
turret	Revolving armoured gun house.
USN	United States Navy.
van	The front of a formation of ships.

Key to flags

For the specification boxes, the national flag that was current at the time of the ship's use is shown.

 Britain

 France

 Germany

 Italy

 Japan

 USA

 USSR

Acknowledgements

The publisher would like to thank the following individuals and picture libraries for the use of their pictures in the book. Every effort has been made to acknowledge the pictures properly, however we apologize if there are any unintentional omissions, which will be corrected in future editions.

l=left, r=right, t=top, b=bottom, m=middle, lm= lower middle

Alinari Archives-Florence:
86t (De Pinto Donazione); 87m Instituto Luce); 87b (De Pinto Donazione); 89mr (De Pinto Donazione).

Australian War Memorial:
14 tr (P00433.001); 23ml (P02018.327); 23mr (P02018.345); 23b (P005999.014).

Cody Images: 5; 6t; 6b; 7tl; 7br; 7r; 8–9; 12t; 12mr; 13tr; 13b; 14tl; 14br; 15tl; 15tr; 15m; 16tl; 16tr; 17t; 17mr; 17br; 22t; 25tr; 28t; 28b; 29t; 29b; 31tl; 31tr; 34tr; 35ml; 35mr; 35m; 36bl; 36br; 37tl; 37ml; 37mr; 38t; 38m; 39t; 39ml; 39mr; 40tl; 40tr; 41tl; 41tr; 41ml; 41lm; 43mr; 43b; 46t; 47tl; 47tr; 47ml; 47lm; 48t; 49t; 49mr; 51t; 51ml; 52t; 52m; 52tl; 52tr; 52ml; 54bl; 55br; 56tl; 56tr; 57t; 57ml; 57mr; 59ml; 61mr; 62tl; 62tr; 63t; 63mr; 64t; 65t; 65b; 66t; 67t; 67ml; 67mr; 68; 69t; 69ml; 69mr; 70; 71t; 71ml; 71mr; 72b; 73m; 73b; 74t; 74bl; 75t; 75m; 75b; 76tr; 76b; 77tr; 77mr; 77b; 78t; 78mr; 79tl; 79tr; 79m; 80t; 81t; 81mr; 81lm; 83tl; 83tr; 83mr; 84tl; 84tr; 85tl; 85mr; 88t; 88bl; 89; 89ml; 90–1; 91tr; 92; 93; 94; 95; 96.

Syd Goodman: 19ml; 19tr; 34t; 42b, 43ml; 44t, 45tl; 45tr; 45mr; 56tl; 56tr; 57tl; 57ml; 57mr; 59ml.

Imperial War Museum Photograph Archive:
18m (HU87084); 26br (A8953); 27tl (Q20352); 27lm (A21164).

Library of Congress:
10m; 11t.

Royal Naval Museum:
19tr; 19ml; 19mr.

US *Missouri* Museum:
60t; 60b; 61tl; 61ml; 95b.

US Naval Historical Center:
1; 2–3; 10t; 11mr; 18tl; 18–19t; 20tl; 20b; 21mr; 21lm; 21br; 22bl; 24t; 25tl; 25mr; 25br; 26t; 27tr; 27ml; 30t; 30m; 31br; 32–3; 49ml; 50t; 51tr; 55tr; 55ml; 55mr; 55bl; 58; 59t; 59mr; 61mr; 63ml; 64ml; 82b.

Index